MY SMALL TOWN

A Memoir
by
YUTANG SANG

Translations by
Dr. Yuan Sang

My Small Town
A Memoir by Yutang Sang
Translations by Yuan Sang

Cover and interior design by Alec Cizak
Photography by Tian Sang

Printed in the United States of America and other countries.

Contact information for Uncle B. Publications, LLC, may be obtained through the website: unclebpublications.com

© 2025 by Yutang Sang

All rights reserved. No parts of this publication may be reproduced in any form or by any means without the prior written consent of the author and/or the publisher.

No generative artificial intelligence (AI) technology was used in the creation of this publication. The publisher expressly prohibits use of this publication for training data for AI technologies or large language models (LLM) for generative purposes.

ISBN-978-1-957034-28-7

First American Printing

My Small Town

序
Preface

I

第一部分 小镇回忆
Memories of the Town

I

第二部分 叙事诗
Narrative Poetry

序

桑玉成

大哥桑玉堂在他耄耋之年写下了他的小镇印记，希望我写个序。说来也很巧，在思考如何写这个序的时间关口，前几天收到家乡寄来的正式出版的《双桥村史》。我为这个村史也写了个序，因为作为家乡人，都希望能够通过一些记忆，来反映我们这个村的历史变迁，来探寻双桥村人的足迹。

实际上，村史是由生活于以及曾经生活于这个村的所有乡亲父老写就的。我想，大哥的这个《我的小镇》出版之后，可以为《双桥村史》增添一个小小的"副本"。到时候我会带着大哥，去双桥村村委会，把这个副本交给村里留存。

大哥说的这个"小镇"叫做"双桥镇"，按照现在的建制，属于张家港市乐余镇下属的一个村，叫"双桥村"。双桥镇以两座桥得名，东市梢的桥和西市梢的桥，所以叫"双桥"。其实用现在的眼光来看，这两座桥完全算不上什么桥，十几米长两三米宽的样子，我印象中早期的时候连个小汽车都无法通行的。但正是两座间隔大概也就百米多距离的小桥，成就了一座百年小镇，绘就了一幅诗情画意的美丽图景。

我们桑家算是这个小镇上的比较早的镇民之一。当然，我的爷爷辈当年是如何从镇江那边南迁到这个小镇的，我完全不知道，因为我出生在这个小镇上，那年已经是1955年了。我大哥长我16岁，尽管他1958年就外出读书后来也一直在外面工作，但是他对于这个小镇的记忆，那是比我要丰厚得多，这个从大哥的《我的小镇》中完全可以看到。

小镇是有深厚文化底蕴的。这里有当地颇有名气的小学和中学。大哥就是在这里读到初中毕业后再到常熟省中读高中，然后从那里考取了北京外贸学院，就是现在的对外经济贸易大学。大哥的人生经历对我有着直接的影响，后来我也就走了读书人的人生之路。

大哥大学毕业之后主动要求去了新疆工作，开始在新疆人民广播电台，后来广播、电视合并，成立广播电视总局，大哥也换了岗位，在新疆电视台做高级编辑。大哥曾担任过新疆人民广播电台、新疆电视台最为重要的节目"新闻联播"的主编。

给我印象最深的是，大哥做事极为敬业也非常专业，他曾经跟我讲过，说做广播编辑与做报纸编辑有什么不同，譬如说，报纸是给人看的，广播是给人听的。读者看报纸的时候，如果一句话没有看明白，他可以停留一会儿、或者回过去再看几遍；但听者听广播的时候，如果一句话没有听清楚，那就没有办法回过头去重新听一遍。当然，现在的技术可以实现重复播放，但过去是不行的。所以，这就对广播编辑提出了非常高的要求。

大哥这些印记主要是围绕家庭成员展开的。一个人，一个家庭的点滴故事，从一个侧面也反映了一个小镇的风风雨雨和时代变迁。细细品味大哥的这些印记，也能为我们找回儿时的乡趣以及那永远也抹不去的乡情。

是为序。

2025年8月写于上海

Preface
Yucheng Sang

My eldest brother, Yutang Sang, wrote his small town imprints in his eighties and asked me to write a preface. Coincidentally, while I was pondering how to write this preface, I received the officially published *History of Shuangqiao Village* from my hometown. I wrote a preface for this village history, because as a fellow villager, I hoped to reflect on the historical changes of our village through our memories and explore the footprints of the people of Shuangqiao.

In fact, the village history is written by all the villagers who have lived in this village. I think that after the publication of my eldest brother's *My Small Town*, it will add to the *History of Shuangqiao Village*. I will then take my eldest brother's book to the Shuangqiao Village Committee to add to the village for pre-servation.

The "small town" my eldest brother writes about here is called "Shuangqiao Town." According to its current administrative system, it is a village called "Shuangqiao Village" under Leyu Town, Zhangjiagang City. Shuangqiao, meaning two bridges, is named after its two bridges: the East Bridge and the West Bridge, hence the name "Shuangqiao." Actually, from today's perspective, these two bridges aren't much of a bridge at all, about a dozen meters long and two or three meters wide. I recall that in the early days, even a small car couldn't pass through them. Yet, it was these two small bridges, only about a hundred meters apart, that shaped this century-old town, painting a picturesque and poetic scene.

Our Sang family was one of the earliest residents of this town. Of course, I have no idea how my grandfather's generation migrated south from Zhenjiang to this place, as I was born here in 1955. My eldest brother is 16 years my senior. Although he left for school in 1958 and has worked away from home ever since, his memories of this town are far richer than mine, as evidenced by his book.

This town has a profound cultural heritage. It boasts some of the most renowned local elementary and middle schools. My eldest brother attended junior high school here, then went on to Changshu Provincial High School. From there, he was admitted to the Beijing Foreign Trade College, now known as the University of International Business and Economics. My eldest brother's life experience had a direct impact on me, and I subsequently followed the path of a scholar.

After graduating from university, my eldest brother volunteered to work in Xinjiang, starting at Xinjiang People's Radio Station. Later, when radio and television merged to form the State Administration of Radio and Television, he became a senior editor at Xinjiang Television Station. He served as the editor-in-chief of "News Broadcast," the most important program for both Xinjiang People's Radio and Television.

What impressed me most was my eldest brother's dedication and professionalism. He once told me the difference between being a radio editor and a newspaper editor. For example, newspapers are for people to read, while radio is for people to listen to. When a reader doesn't understand a sentence in a newspaper, they can pause or go back and read it again. But when a listener listens to the radio, if they don't hear a sentence clearly, there's no way to go back and listen again. Of course, today's technology allows for repeat playback, but that wasn't possible in the past. Therefore, this places extremely high demands on broadcast editors.

My brother's traces primarily revolve around family members. The stories of one individual and one family reflect, from a perspective, the ups and downs of a small town and the changing times. Carefully savoring these traces can also help us rediscover the joys of childhood and the enduring nostalgia for home.

Shanghai, August 2025

第一部分 小镇回忆
Memories of the Town

一．重回双桥镇

回到阔别七十余年的故乡，生我养我的双桥镇，心情特别激动和复杂，难以用语言表述清楚。

踏上硬路面的街道，看着街道两旁的凉棚档和一溜平房，那种既亲切又陌生的感觉顿时油然而生。想当年街上行人如织，来来往往，热闹非常，如今却是冷落荒凉，难见人影，偶有一、两人走动，也大多是老头、老太。以往街道两边的商铺，也大多大门紧闭，中间偶有一、两个小商店也是可怜兮兮的样子，门可罗雀，但仍在那里硬撑着小镇的名字，坚守着它的岁月。

双桥镇只有一条东西向的主街道，全长或有一、两里，中间有一条河港穿过，上架一座木桥，把东西街道连接在一起。如今这座木桥已被水泥路面所代替。街道东西两端建有庙宇，东有城隍庙，西有关帝庙。可以想象当初的小镇设计者和建设者用心良苦，敬请神灵来保佑全镇生意兴隆，平安繁荣。当然，这也是全镇商家和居民的心愿。如今城隍庙旧址已改建为住家，西面的关帝庙依然存在，庙里还有和尚住持。据说他们还经常外出为丧家充当吹鼓手，敲木鱼，念经，超度亡灵。庙前的银杏树已有百年历史，依然摇曳着金黄色的树叶，树下还依然散落着银杏的果实。记得小时候我们几个小伙伴常到这里捡拾白果。这棵银杏树应该还认识我们吧，它在风中摆动的枝叶不是在向我们挥手致意吗？

原先西街的小作坊较多。李家的磨坊，总见蒙着双眼的小毛驴围着磨盘转圈，不停地转，永远转不完。倪木匠推着刨子，木花朵朵永远开不败。曹家的豆腐坊里永远是热气腾腾，飘散着豆腐的香味。裁衣王师傅脖子上挂着皮尺，耳朵上夹着粉块，不是量身裁衣，就是坐在那里缝制衣服，后来还添置了缝纫机和拷边机，"哒哒哒"的机器声使裁缝店增添了一点现代节奏感。

西街上还有赵家客栈，迎接南来北往的过客。张家的粮店，有米、有麦、有面，解决全镇大人小孩的吃饭问题。还有两家早餐店，供应烧饼、油条、馒头。此外，还有脚踏车行，修车、打气、配零件。双桥镇唯一的十字街头或叫十字路口就在西街。在十字路口有一家较有名气的商店，那就是桑义隆茶食店。这家茶食店是从镇江丹徒搬迁过来的，租用了施家的两间门面，自产自销各类茶食。桑家茶食大致分为三类：一是烘烤类，二是剪炸类，三是糖果类。烘烤类有月饼、鸡蛋糕、老虎脚爪、脆饼、广东饼、桃酥、奶糕、喜糕（云片糕）、芝麻饼等。煎炸类有馓子、油绞绞（音gao，北方人称麻花）、糖枣（北方人称江米条）等。糖果类有寸金糖、冬瓜糖等。上述这些食品、糖果如今保留下来的已经不多，大多已经失传，在市场上销声匿迹了。要特别提一下的是奶糕，这是当时当地的婴儿食品。在当时当地没有牛奶和奶粉的情况下，婴儿在会吃饭之前，除了吃母乳，就是吃奶糕了。当时桑家生产的奶糕营养卫生，经济实惠，宝宝们爱吃，深受产妇们的喜爱和欢迎。吃奶糕，成为当地几代人童时的共同回忆。可以说，桑义隆茶食店在这方面还有点特色！

在桑家茶食店的对面是冯家的鞋店，既卖鞋又为他人绱鞋。当年冯师傅总是坐在矮凳上，双手拉着长长的鞋底线来回穿梭，忙个不停。一双双鞋就在他的手上成型。

从这十字路口朝南约五百米左右的街道有着另样的风景。首先是冯医生开的诊所，这是小镇唯一的一家医疗诊所。冯医生医术精湛，医德高尚，甚得当地群众的一致称赞。当时有位姓朱的患者，腿上生疮多年不愈，除了疼痛还流脓不止，非常痛苦。家人把他从数十里远的家中送到冯医生这里治疗。冯医生把病人留在家里吃住，亲自为病人洗涤疮口，上药换药，不厌其烦，不怕脏累。经过一个多月的精心治疗，病人终于痊愈，高高兴兴地走了回去。后来，他给冯家诊所送来一块大匾，上书"还我健康"，高高地挂在了诊所的墙上。我那时上小学，上学放学每次路过诊所的时候，总要瞄一眼这块大匾，这在我心中留下了不可磨灭的印象。

在南街，还值得一提的是榨油厂，那是施财主的儿孙辈大学毕业后回乡开办的。这是双桥镇有史以来开办的第一家工厂。当时，机器的轰鸣声，提升了小镇的兴旺和活力。四邻八乡的黄豆源源不断地运到厂里，工厂榨出来的豆油一桶桶地向各地分发。厂前的街面上时有散落的黄豆，那时候我们一群小伙伴们常来捡拾，如获至宝。但不知道好端端的一个榨油厂为什么没有继续开下去，也不知道什么时候关闭的。如今这里已成了几家住户了。

西街还有两家较大的商店（商号），那就是杨家森福昌的纸店和黄家裕泰丰的布店。此外，还有陆家的书店兼文具店，盖的是两层小楼，堪称镇上第一楼，这在整个双桥镇是绝无仅有的。当时镇北有崇实中学，镇南有双桥小学。中小学生离不开书店、文具店。他们常来光顾，非常闹猛，很是兴旺，这也是我学生时代留连忘返的去处。在当年连接东西街的木桥的桥东头，是许师傅开的肉铺，他个子矮小，但很壮实。他挥刀剁肉，一刀一个准。老板娘干练利索，收钱找钱，忙而不乱，快而无差错。两口子经营肉铺生意兴隆，日子过得殷实，可惜膝下无儿无女。如今这里不仅人去，房屋也没有了踪影。

当年东街刘家的药店给我留下了难忘的印象。装有各种各样药材的一个个小抽屉，摆满了整整一堵墙。药店学徒经常坐在那里，双脚踩着一个铁饼似的东西，在铁槽子里来回转动，这是在碾碎磨细药材。院子里摆着一个个筛子，里面晾晒着从当地采购来的药材，如蝉衣、蚯蚓皮、芦根等。

药店对面是张家的染布店。当年，他家后院搭建了高高的木头架子，上面晾晒着整匹染成各种颜色的布料，其中黑色、蓝色的居多。布料迎风飘扬，像一面面彩旗，是小镇一道多彩的风景。人们在远远的地方就能望见，很是醒目。

离染布店不远就是小镇一家较大的理发店。当年我喜欢到这里来理发，特别是在酷热难耐的夏天。夏天，这家理发店在店里吊一个一米见方的棉帘，上面装有滑轮，用绳子牵引着。学徒一拉一松绳子，使棉帘来回摆动，起到扇风作用，使顾客也包括理发师感到阵阵凉意。这在当时没有电风扇和空调的情况下，不失为降温的一个创举。

当年走到东市梢附近，远远就能闻见一缕缕清香。原来这里是顾家的香店。他们把香料等原料调成面团状，然后挤压成面条状的香，放在排门板上晒干，最后制成线香、棒香和盘香等，再批发给商贩们出售。这是当时当地人家敬神祭祖的必用品。今天香店的房屋还在，破旧斑驳，空关着，顾家人已不知去向。我使劲吸着空气，似乎在寻找往年那缕熟悉的香气。

双桥镇繁荣过，兴旺过，但也经历了两次较大的劫难。两座庙宇的神灵也无能为力。一次是抗战胜利前夕，一股土匪趁战乱之机洗劫了双桥镇，还施行绑票。还有一次是解放前夕的一个春节，国民党反动派兵败如山倒，从苏北败退到江南，双桥镇首当其冲，又被洗劫一空。伤痕累累的双桥镇从此一蹶不振，日渐败落下去。但最终迎来了解放，获得了新生！

　　七十多年过去了，现在的双桥镇已经没有了以往的繁华和喧闹。街道两旁原先的商铺大多不复存在，大门紧闭。时有两层小楼挤在中间或耸立在后院。在偶有的开着门的门口，坐着一个老头或老太，望着街道发呆，或眯着眼睛打盹，似乎沉浸在深深的回忆之中。曾经繁荣过、兴旺过的双桥镇，今天已经被更加繁荣、更加兴旺的乐余镇所取而代之。

今日小镇/Today's town

I. Back to Shuangqiao Town

Back in my hometown Shuangqiao after more than 70 years, I was especially excited with a complicated feeling that was difficult to express.

Stepping on the hard paved street, looking at the cool sheds and a row of one-floor houses on either side, familiar and unfamiliar feelings filled my heart. In my memory, there were always a lot of pedestrians on the street, coming and going, very lively. Now, it seemed barren, hardly anybody to be seen—only a few every now and then—mostly the elderly. The stores that used to stand on the street were now mostly closed. Occasionally, there was one or two that were still open, but looking miserable, as if birds could land there without being scared off. The dotted operating stores struggled to uphold the integration of the town.

Shuangqiao Town has only one main street running west to east, for about one mile. A river crossed the town in the middle, over which there was a wooden bridge connecting the west and the east sides. Nowadays, the wooden bridge has been replaced by a concrete one. On both sides, there are temples—Town Temple on the east and Guandi Temple on the west. You can imagine the intention of the designer and creator of the town—recruiting the gods and spirits to bless the whole town to be prosperous and peaceful. Of course, this is also the wish of all the businessmen and residents in the town. Now, the Town Temple has already been repurposed into a residency. The Guandi Temple is still there with practicing monks. It's said that they often go out to play instruments, knocking on their wood fish, chanting scriptures, and ferrying the dead. The ginkgo tree in the front yard of the temple has been there for about a hundred years. It still sways its golden leaves, nuts scattering on the ground. I remember when I was little, my friends and I would come here to pick the ginkgo nuts. It should still remember us. Aren't the swaying leaves waving to and greeting us?

The west side used to hold more small workshops. The Li's mill witnessed the blind-folded donkey walking endlessly around and around the grinding disc. Carpenter Ni pushed the plane, wooden "flowers" blossoming and never withering. Cao's tofu store always had a steamy aroma. On tailor Wang's neck hung a tape, his ear holding a chalk. He was either measuring and cutting the cloth or sitting there sewing. Later, he got a sewing machine and an edging machine, the sound of "tatata" added some modern rhythm to the tailor store.

There was also Zhao's Inn to welcome tourists from all directions. Zhang's grain store provided the town with its rice, wheat, and flour. In addition, there was also a bike store that repaired bikes, pumped air, and provided parts. The only crossroads in the town was on the west side. There was a famous store—The Sang Yilong snack store. Having relocated here from Dantu, Zhenjiang, it rented two street rooms from the Shi's and sold various self-made snacks. Their snacks mainly fell in three categories: baked, deep fried, and candied. Baked snacks were mooncakes, egg cakes, tiger paws, crispy pancakes, Guangdong pancakes, walnut crisps, milk cakes, celebrating cakes (layered cakes), and sesame cakes, etc. Deep fried snacks included Sanzi, twists, and date candy (Jiangmi strips in the north), etc. Candied snacks were Inch-Gold, winter melon candy, etc. A few of the above-mentioned snacks have been passed down while most are lost in time. A special shout-out goes to the milk cake, a local baby food. At that time when there was no milk or milk powder, babies ate milk cake in addition to breast milk before they ate normal solid food. The Sang's milk cake was nutritious, healthy, and inexpensive. The babies loved it and moms too. Eating milk cake has become a common memory for several generations.

Opposite the Sang's snack store was Feng's shoe store. They sold and mended shoes. Back then, Mr. Feng was always seen sitting on a bench with his hands busy shuffling the shoe threads. One after another, pairs of shoes were born of his hands.

The 500-meter street to the south of the crossroads bore the same scenery. First, there was Feng's Clinic, the only medical service spot in town. Dr. Feng had great medical skills and a noble heart. He was highly praised by the locals. There once was a patient surnamed Zhu whose painful leg got sores with pus constantly oozing out. His family sent him to Dr. Feng from home about five miles away. Accommodating Zhu in his own home, Dr. Feng cleaned his wounds, applied medicine, changed medicine in person without any complaints. After more than a month's careful treatment, Zhu finally recovered and walked back home happily. Later, he sent Dr. Feng a big plaque on which was written, "Rendered my Health Back." It was put high up on the clinic's wall. I was in elementary school at that time. Every time I passed the clinic, I would always catch a glimpse of the plaque, which carved an indelible impression in my heart.

On the south street, there also sat the oil mill established by the landlord Shi's later generation after they graduated from college. This was the first ever factory in the history of Shuangqiao Town. At that time, the roaring of the machines represented the prosperity and livelihood of the little town. Soybeans from all directions were sent to the factory like a steady stream, while barrels of squeezed oil were distributed to various places. The street in front of the factory saw scattered soybeans. Little kids like us used to come here to pick them up like gems. Nobody knows when or why the oil mill was closed. Now, several residents live here.

There were two bigger stores on the west street—the Senfuchang paper store of the Yang's and the Yutaifeng cloth store of the Huang's. Also, there was a book and stationary store of the Lu's, which was a two-story building, the first ever in town. This was also the only two-story building in Shuangqiao Town. At that time, the north of the town had the Chongshi Middle School and the south, the Shuangqiao Elementary School. Since schoolers couldn't go without books or stationery, their frequent visits to the store made it prosperous. This was also my loitering place. On the east of the wooden bridge that connected the West and East streets, there was the butcher shop of Mr. Xu's. He was short but stout and his meat cutting was precise. His wife was skilled and neat, receiving payment and giving out change. She was busy but never made mistakes. The couple had a good business, a wealthy life, but what a pity, no kids. Now, there is no one there, not even the house.

The impressive pharmacy of the Zhao's sat on the east street. Little drawers filled with all kinds of Chinese traditional medicine ingredients occupied an entire wall. The apprentice sat there, his feet spinning on an iron grinder. He was grinding the herbs. All kinds of sieves were set in the yard drying herbs bought from all over the place, such as cicada sloughs, silkworms, and reed roots, etc.

Opposite the pharmacy was the Liu's cloth dyeing store. In his back yard, there were high wooden shelves where dyed clothes dried, mainly black and blue. The clothes fluttered in the wind like flags, forming a colorful scenery. It could be seen from afar, very striking to the eye.

Not far from the cloth dyeing store, there was a relatively bigger barber shop in town. I used to go there to have my hair cut, especially in the steaming hot summer. In the heat, the shop hung a one-meter-squared-size cotton-stuffed curtain which had a pulley string. The apprentice pulled and loosened it to make the curtain swing back and forth to create wind. Both the customers and barbers could feel the coolness. As there were no electric fans or air conditioners, this was a pretty good innovation.

If you walked to the east side of the street at that time, you could smell wisps of fragrance from afar. It was from the incense store of the Gu's. They mixed the spices to a dough, squeezed them into incense sticks, dried them on the row door panels, and finally made incense threads, sticks, and coils. They sold them to the retail stores. Incenses are necessities for local people to worship the gods and ancestors. Today, the house of the incense store is still there, but closed, leaving the Gu's nowhere to be seen. I take long breaths, hoping to catch a whiff of the familiar fragrance.

Shuangqiao Town was prosperous, lively, but also suffered two disasters which couldn't have been helped even by the deities in the two temples. One disaster was on the eve of the victory of the Anti-Japanese War, when a group of bandits took advantage of the war and robbed the town. They also kidnapped some people. The other time was at the Spring Festival before the liberation. After the Kuomingtang reactionaries were defeated like falling mountains, they retreated from the north of Jiangsu to the south, on the route of which Shuangqiao Town was first hit and robbed every and each way. The badly wounded town slumped after that, although finally it got liberated and reborn.

More than 70 years passed. Shuangqiao Town today has lost its prosperity and livelihood. The streetside stores are mostly closed, no longer busy. Once every few feet, there are two-story residencies sitting among them or in the back yard. Occasionally, there are now open stores where an old man or woman sits. They either fix their eyesight on the street or doze off, as if immersing in their deep memories. Shuangqiao Town that used to be prosperous and lively, has been replaced by the Leyu Town which is more prosperous and lively.

小镇理发店/The survived barber shop

二. 农家"三宝"

张家港北部沿长江一带，包括乐余镇以北的双桥镇、东界港，西至老海县以东的十二圩港、西界港，东至六干河直至常阴沙农场，这一片江滩平原，时称常阴沙，当地人称"沙上"。当时居住在这里的人自称或他称为"沙上人"。

这里的居民绝大多数务农，他们既勤劳又聪明，充分利用本地自然资源制作各种各样的用品，以适应生活，改善自己的生存和生活条件。资源中最常用也最常见的有这样三种东西，我称之为"三宝"，那就是：芦苇、竹子、稻草。

芦苇，这里俗称芦头，苇头，多年生草本植物。这里沟河港湾纵横交错，更有广阔的长江江滩，到处生长着茂密的芦苇，自然野生，不用施肥，更不用浇灌，其从穗至根，全身都是宝，都有不同的用处。芦花可制作暖暖的芦花婆鞋。茎中空，光滑，我们所说的芦头，就是指这一部分。它可编席，也可以造纸。芦叶披针形，当地用来包粽子。芦根含水份，还甜津津的，小朋友们把它们当甘蔗吃。其实它还是一味中药材，可制作利尿剂和清热解毒剂。

解放前直至上世纪五、六十年代，这里的农村住房大多是草屋，即茅草房。房子四周墙壁，大多是芦头编成的篱笆墙，房顶衬底的也是用芦头编织而成。一间间的房子中间也大多用篱笆隔开。可以这样说，当时当地的茅草房百分之九十的原材料来自于芦苇。想当年，我们一家八口（父母和六个兄弟姐妹）就是蜗居在两间茅草房里，长达十年之久！我永远感念大自然的恩赐，感念亭亭玉立默默奉献的芦苇！

在乡下，几乎家家都有至少一顶榰子，榰子主要用芦头编成。首先剥净芦头的外皮，粗细适中，笔笔直，然后用事先搓好的细麻绳，分成近十个档次，把芦头一根根编进去，最后形成五米左右长的榰子。不用时卷起来，用时先打行，后把榰子放在上面发开，可在上面晒棉花，晒被褥衣物，放个晒垫晒粮食等等。给我儿时印象深刻的是年末家中蒸馒头时，在场院铺好榰子，一笼笼蒸熟的馒头翻倒在上面，诱人的香味随着腾腾热气在榰子上升起并弥漫开来，此情此景使人终生难忘。

第二宝是竹子，当地人称为竹头，竹子禾本科，多年生植物。竹竿木质化，质地坚硬，用途非常广，可供建筑用，也可作造纸原料，还可编织各种生活用具。幼芽就是通常说的竹笋，当蔬菜吃，味道鲜美。当地农村几乎家家户户都有一个小竹园，大多种在房屋后院、河边、岸边等犄角旮里，不占耕地，也不影响其它农作物的生长。

那时候，乡下砌的大多是草房子，盖草房子就离不了竹头。比如房檩大多用较粗的毛竹，椽子也大多用竹头，至于边墙（即芦芭墙）和山墙（也为芦芭墙）的连接也用的是竹头劈削而成的蔑丝。

竹头用处最多也最常见的是用竹头劈削成蔑丝后编织的各种各样的用品，如用来存放粮食谷物的盘篮，粗细不一的筛子，大大小小的竹篮，淘米用的淘箩，夏天睡觉用的竹席，晒粮食的晒垫等等。特别是竹篮，用处可大了。到田间地头挑菜挑草拾棉花用它，上街买鱼买肉买菜用它，甚至走亲访友携带礼物礼品也用它。现在看来，这些竹篮要比现在的塑料袋环保得多，也经济得多。

就是种植蔬菜也得用竹头，搭个黄瓜棚、丝瓜棚、豇豆棚等。可以这样说，当时当地的农家，房上屋下，场里院外，处处都有竹头的身影。

这里农家的第三宝就是稻草（当地人称为稻柴），稻草就是稻子成熟脱粒后剩下的稻秆。其用途在当时是非常广泛的，除了通常用作燃料、饲料等外，乡下最大的用处就是用来盖房子。解放前，直至解放初期的五、六十年代，你只要一到乡下农村，首先映入眼帘的就是一家家的茅草房，这草屋的草就是稻草，屋顶屋面上铺的是一层层厚厚的稻草，稻草上面用一条条稻草绳穿上芦头和竹头，如网似的遮住稻草。每年新稻收割之后更换一次，到时崭新的金黄色的新稻草使茅草房焕然一新，在阳光下闪着耀眼的光芒，这才是名副其实的蓬荜生辉！

这时节，乡民们用新稻草铺床，放在褥子下面，睡在上面既柔软又暖和，还接地气，可与现今的席梦思相媲美。

在农村，每家每户都有大大小小的缸、甏之类的器皿，用来存放粮食、豆类等农产品。但缸、甏都没有盖子，于是这里的农民就用稻草扎，当地人称之谓"草盖头"。

稻草更常用的是稻草绳，农户用精选的稻草，搓成粗细不等的绳子，能够派到很多的用场。如果需要很粗的稻草绳，通常需要三到四个人的合作。如果绳子是两股的，就是两人分别用手握好稻草，并不断地往里面添放，另一人用一种人工做成的摇杆，不停地摇动，就拧成了两股的绳子。如果是三股的，就要有三个人分别用手握好稻草，这里的冬天很冷，而且没有任何取暖设备，为了让婴幼儿安全度过寒冬，乡下的能工巧匠用稻草为主要原料编扎草窠。草窠下面放个火钵头（或烘缸），小朋友站在上面非常暖和，为妈妈们解忧、减负，很受她们的欢迎。

　　乡下农民经常用稻草搓绳、绞绳、串篱笆、搭黄瓜棚、豇豆棚、捆秸秆等等，随时随地都用得上。

　　芦头、竹头和稻草，这农家"三宝"，看起来太平常，太不起眼了，也不值钱，但对当地的农民们来说，却是他们生产和生活中不可或缺的忠实伴侣。随着科技的进步和经济的发展，这"三宝"如今已渐渐淡出人们的视线乃至记忆。

梿子 / Lianzi, used to sun bathe various items

II. "The Three Treasures" in On-Sand

The plain area along the Yangtze River in the north of Zhangjiagang, including Shuangqiao Town, East Border Harbor to the north of Leyu Town, the west side reaching the Twelfth Dike Harbor, West Border Harbor to the east of Old Sea County, the east side getting to Six Stem River until the Chang-Yin-Sand Ranch, was called Chang-Yin-Sand, locally nicknamed "On-Sand." The residents there are called "the On-Sand-ers."

The vast majority of them farm to live. Diligent and bright, they take advantage of local resources to make various kinds of doo-dads to adapt life and to improve their survival and living conditions. The most commonly used and seen among the resources, which I call "The Three Treasures," are: reed, bamboo, and straw.

Reed, locally called reed-head, is a perennial herb. With ditches, rivers, harbors, and bays crisscrossing each other, plus the vast area of the Yangtze River beach, lush reed stands everywhere, naturally growing, no need for any fertilization or irrigation. Yet, from the reed ear down to the root, every and each part of it is precious and can be used for various purposes. The reed flower can be made into warm shoes. The stem, so-called reed-head, being hollow and smooth, can be weaved into bed sheets or made into paper. The lanceolate leaves are used to wrap zongzi, a traditional food for the Dragon Boat Festival. The juicy reed root, kind of sweet, therefore, is like sugar canes for kids. It's also used in Traditional Chinese Medicine to make diuretics and heat-clearing and detoxifying agents.

From before Mao's time to the 1950s and 60s, most of the rural houses here were thatched cottages. The walls were like fences, mostly weaved with the reed-head. The roof underlayment was also a reed-head weave. Houses were additionally separated by reed-head fences. You may comfortably say that 90% of the raw material for the local cottages then was from the reed. In those days, my family of eight (my parents and six siblings) dwelled in two of those thatched cottage rooms for as long as 10 years. I am forever grateful for nature's gift—the stand-still, silently dedicated reed.

In our villages, almost every household has at least one lianzi (picture on p.13), mainly weaved by reed-head. First, peel the skin of the reed-head that is of the appropriate size and straight. Then, weave the reed-heads at about 10 equally-separated spots with hemp ropes that have been twisted together. The lianzi is usually five meters long with the weaved reed-heads. When it's not used, it's rolled up. When it's needed, you make a simple scaffold before unrolling it on the top. You can use it to sunbathe cotton, clothes and quilts, and grains with a fine sun pad above the lianzi. What impressed me the most in my childhood was the bun making at the end of each year. You lay out the lianzi in the yard, then pour the many baskets of newly steamed buns onto it. The tempting/luring aroma, together with the hot steam, rises and spreads in the cold winter air. The scene is unforgettable.

The second treasure is bamboo, locally called bamboo-head, bamboo Poaceae, perennial. When the bamboo stem lignifies, it is hardened and can be used for a variety of purposes: in construction, as an ingredient in paper making, or weaved into different living utensils. The young buds, commonly known as bamboo shoots, are a delicious vegetable. In the local villages, almost every household has a little bamboo garden, mostly in the backyard, alongside the river, or on the bank, places that are not regular farmland and where bamboo doesn't affect crops' growth.

At that time, the most commonly seen houses were thatches that can't manage without bamboo-head. For example, the purlin is mostly made of thick bamboo, so is the rafter. As to the joints of the side wall (i.e., the fence wall) and the gable (also the fence wall), the bamboo skin peel chopped from bamboo is used.

The bamboo skin peel, the most multi-functioned and commonly used, can be weaved into all kinds of utensils, such as flat baskets for spreading grains, sieves of different sizes, all kinds of baskets, dense sieves for rice rinsing, bed sheets for summer nights, and sun pads for drying grains, etc. Especially the bamboo baskets, what many roles they play! They tag along to the field for you to pick vegetables, to weed, and to pick cotton. They go with you to the market for fish, meat, and other grocery. They even carry your gifts to your friends and relatives. It seems that they are much more environmentally friendly and more economical than plastic bags.

Even when you grow vegetables, you need bamboo to build a cucumber shed, a silk melon shed, and a cowpea shed, etc. You may say that, at that time, for the local household, on the house, in the house, in the yard, outside the yard, there's bamboo everywhere.

The third treasure here is rice straw, the plant after rice grains are harvested. Its usage is very extensive. Other than fuel or feed, the biggest function is its application in making houses. Before Mao's time, even into the 1950s and 60s, once you arrived at the village, the first sight was thatched houses. The thatch is the rice straw that is layered tightly and thickly and then covered by a net of reed-head and bamboo-head enforced with straw ropes within. The thatcher is changed every year after the harvest of new rice. The newly changed yellow rice straw, shining under the sky, gives the whole house a brand-new look.

During this time, villagers use the new rice straw to put under their mattress quilt for the bed. Sleeping on that is both soft and warm and makes one feel grounded, which can be favorably compared to the modern spring mattress.

In the village, every household has containers of all sizes like cylinders and urns to store grains and beans. But they don't have lids. Therefore, the local people tie the rice straw together to make them, locally called straw covers.

A more common usage of straw is the rope that is made of selected rice straw by twisting it. Thick or thin, it can be used on all kinds of occasions. If you need to make thick ropes, cooperation of three or four people is needed. If it's two strings, then two people hold the hay while adding more into it. Another person then uses a man-made appliance called a rocker to spin the strings into a rope. If it's three strings, then you need three people to hold the hay for twisting.

Winter here is very cold. When you don't have any heating system, the craftsmen make straw nests for young kids to safely weather the chill. A covered fire bowl is placed under the nests for the babies to get warmth, which relieves moms' worries and burden.

The villagers here often use the straw to make ropes which apply almost everywhere: fences, cucumber and bean scaffolds, and tying straw, etc.

Reed-head, bamboo-head, and rice straw, the three treasures to us villagers, look so common and plain, but are indispensable, loyal companions in our life and work. With the advancement of technology and development of the economy, the three treasures have been fading out of people's eyesight, and even memory.

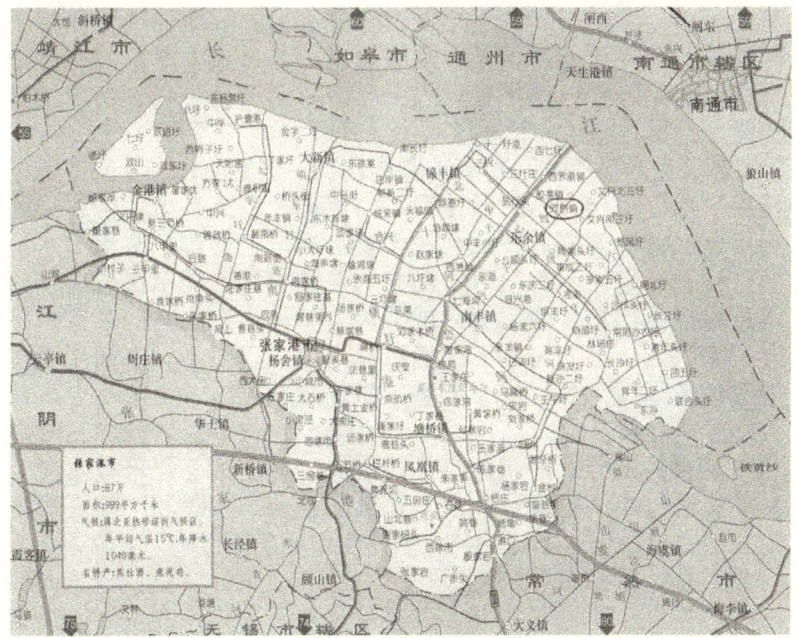

张家港地图东北部的双桥镇（已圈出）/ Shuangqiao Town, circled on the northeast of Zhangjiagang city

三．取暖土办法

在双桥镇及其周围的十里八村，每逢寒冬腊月，西老北风从长江江面上呼啸吹来，河面结冰，路面泛白坚硬，草木簌簌发抖，房檐挂着一排排长长的冰凌。这时节，如何御寒取暖成了当地人们极为关注和操心的一大课题。

这里的劳动者是勤劳的，也是智慧的。上世纪五、六十年代，在这里没有电网不通电的情况下，人们发挥自己的聪明才智，利用本地的自然资源，精心制作御寒取暖用品。这里有广阔的江滩和纵横交错的港湾河道，适宜芦苇的生长。芦苇，属禾本科，多年生草木，夏秋季开花，呈圆锥花，序长10至40厘米，小穗含四至七个小花，花色呈灰白色。花序除了制作扫帚外，就是用来制作冬天穿的鞋子，当地人称为芦花婆鞋。芦花如棉花般暖和，其纤维比棉花长而结实。这里的手艺人利用芦花和稻草加工制作芦花婆鞋。那时候，每到秋末冬初，在双桥镇的早市上，能经常看见手艺人挑着一担芦花婆鞋出售，鞋子尺码有大有小，就连三、四岁小朋友穿的都有。我还清楚记得我小时候第一次穿这鞋的情景：双眼紧紧盯着母亲把厚厚的棉鞋垫塞进鞋里，一针一线把鞋口沿上布条，刚一完工我立马抢过鞋子穿上，顿时感到一股暖意从脚底升起。

御寒取暖的重点关注对象当属婴幼儿。这里在几代人的成长过程中，都会有自己小时候站草窠的经历。草窠是当地劳动人民利用自然资源御寒取暖的又一创造。当地普遍种植水稻，水稻的秸秆，当地人称为稻草（稻柴）。农家利用稻草搓成绳子，用草绳捆扎稻草，最后盘织成下大上小一米高左右的草窠。下方呈喇叭形，上方呈圆形，能稳稳地放在地面上。中间用小木棍或竹子隔开，其上放个棉垫，供幼儿站立。下面放一个火钵头，就是在钵头里放砻糠、木屑之类，约占钵头体积的三分之二，其余的三分之一压上火热的豆萁、棉花萁等柴禾或木炭，其热量通过中间的隔层，涌上草窠的上层，可暖和站在上面的幼儿。整个冬天这里的幼儿大多是在草窠里度过的。

"矮婆婆，眼睛多，吃红饭，屙黑鯢"，儿时猜到这则谜语时的兴奋心情至今还记忆犹新，谜底就是本地人称为的烘缸。烘缸用金属制成，大多是铜制品，盖子上均匀地布满洞眼，就是谜语中说的"眼睛多"。里面的填充物类似火钵头，烘缸大都用来暖和手、脚，也可烘热、烘干婴幼儿的衣服、鞋袜和尿布等。那时候，这里家家户户都是用灶烧饭，冬天天寒地冻，家庭主妇烧好早饭后会马上用灶膛里炽热的柴烬把烘缸、火钵头来个"吐故纳新"，倒尽前一天的柴灰，换上新的砻糠和柴烬。其保暖的时间可持续十个小时，中间用小锹翻几次，也可添些柴烬（烧煮午餐时）。

那个时节，晚上睡觉我们小时候最怕也最难忘的一幕那，就是脱掉棉衣裤只穿单衣裤钻进被窝时那种冰冷刺骨的感觉。父母们为了让自己的孩子睡觉有个温暖的被窝，就使用一种叫"汤婆子"的来取暖。汤婆子用金属（太多是铜）制成，呈扁圆形，用时灌满开水（沸水），旋紧盖子，放进被窝，不一会儿，被窝里热热的，人钻进去倍感温暖和舒服，不久就会进入甜美的梦乡。用汤婆子取暖，效果好，很方便，还安全，持续时间长。

随着社会、经济的发展和科技的进步，上述的御寒取暖办法已经淹没在历史的烟雨中，如今只留在了老一辈人的记忆深处。

寒冷的冬天/Cold winter

III. Local Methods of Heating

In Shuangqiao Town and its peripheral villages, in cold winters, northwestern winds soar from the frozen surface of the Yangtze River. The roads look grey and are rock solid. Plants shiver. Long icicles hang down from the edges of the houses. In such times, how to keep warm becomes a great concern of the locals.

The village people are industrious and clever. In the 1950's and 1960's, there was no electricity, yet they took advantage of the local natural resources to carefully make warming gigs. Here, the vast river beaches and crisscrossing harbor channels provided a suitable environment for reeds to prosper. Reeds, Poaceae, perennial, bloom in panicles in summer and autumn, 10 to 40 centimeters long. Their spikelets contain four to seven small flowers, gray white. The inflorescence is used, in addition to make brooms, to make winter shoes, locally called Reed Flower Grandma shoes. The reed flower is as warm as cotton, but with fibers longer and sturdier than cotton. At that time, every end of fall and beginning of winter, in the morning market of Shuangqiao Town, you often saw craftsmen carrying a stand of that kind of shoes for sale. The sizes varied, even those for toddlers. I remember clearly the first time I put on mine: my eyes were fixed on mom who put thick cotton insoles in the shoes. She then stitched along the shoe opening with a long stripe. The moment she finished, I grabbed them and put them on, feeling the instant warmth steaming up from my feet.

The key groups for the concern of keeping warm, of course, are the babies and infants. Several generations of growing up here experienced sitting in the straw nest. Straw nests are another creation of utilizing natural resources to keep warm by the local people. Rice is universally grown here. The stem of rice is called rice grass or rice straw. The rural people twist the straw into ropes which is used to bind straw stacks to weave into a one-meter-high nest, smaller on top and bigger on the bottom. The bottom, looking like a trumpet, with the round top, can stay on the ground stably. The middle is separated by a little stick or bamboo on which they put a cotton cushion for kids to stand on. Below the separation placed a fire bowl, two-thirds of which contain stuff like chaff and shaving, the rest of which is pressed with burning beanstalks or cotton stalks. The heat created can go up to the top to warm the kid standing on it through the separation layer. For the whole winter, young kids mostly spend their time in this kind of straw nest.

"A many-eyed short granny who eats red and dumps black." The memory of excitement for solving the riddle in childhood is still fresh. The answer is a warming cylinder. It is made of metal, mostly copper, with holes evenly spread on the lid, referred by the "many eyes" in the riddle. The inside stuffing is similar to the fire bowl. Warming cylinders are mostly used to warm hands and feet, sometimes also to warm or dry babies' clothes, shoes, and diapers, etc. At that time, every household used wood-fired ovens for cooking. In freezing cold winter, after cooking breakfast, housewives would replace the stuffing in the fire bowl and warming cylinder with the remaining log and fire in the oven and change the chaff and shaving. The warmth can last up to 10 hours. In the meantime, you could stir it with a small spade or add more wood during lunch time.

In those winters, the scariest and most unforgettable moment in sleeping for a child was the icy, burn-penetrating feeling when you took off the heavy clothes and sneak into the quilt. In order to let their kids have a warm quilt nest, parents used a kind of hot water bottle called Water Pozi. It is made of metal, mostly copper, round and flat. When using it, you fill it with hot water (best boiling), tighten the lid, and put it into the quilt. Soon, the nest is warm. You feel warm and comfortable when you get in there and soon fall asleep. Using Water Pozi to keep warm is effective, convenient, safe, and long lasting.

With the development of society and economy, and the advancement of science and technology, the aforementioned warming methods have already been drowned in the smoke and rain of history, only staying in the deep memory of the older generation.

四．祭灶

过了腊八，新年越来越近了。进入腊月二十，似乎来到了年的脚下。腊月二十四，我们乡下几乎每家都要祭灶，即祭祀灶王爷（我们乡下俗称为灶家菩萨）。

我们乡下地处长江下游的江边上，这里的居民主要来自江苏北部和崇明岛，被称为"江北人"和"崇明人"。他们的方言和生活方式相互融合，经过百多年的相处，如今已不分彼此，都成为当地人了。

这里每家都砌有一个做饭菜用的炉灶，柴禾用的是稻、麦、玉米、黄豆、油菜等农作物的秸秆。灶灰最后用来肥田，算是一个循环，很环保的。这里的一个习俗，就是腊月二十四，每家都要祭祀灶家菩萨，就是祭灶。似乎每家有吃有穿，全依仗着自家灶家菩萨的保佑和赐舍。

祭灶仪式其实非常简单。这一天的晚饭，每家都要烧赤豆饭（赤豆和大米）。这里的人称为"烧廿四夜饭"。赤豆每家都有，自己种的。烧的蔬菜就是青菜烧豆腐。开饭后盛的第一碗赤豆饭、第一碗青菜豆腐，都要放在灶头上灶王爷（菩萨）画像的面前，一直到除夕才撤去。灶王爷画像的两边还贴有一副对联，上联是"上天言好事"，下联是"下界保平安"。灶头上点亮两枝红蜡烛，燃着一把香，家人随即叩头跪拜，既是对灶王爷一年来的保佑表示感谢，又是对来年的祈福。

小时候目睹祭灶只觉得有趣，不知其所以然。现在想来还挺有意思的。为什么要烧赤豆米饭呢？老人们解释说，是让灶王爷吃饭时，只顾数碗里的赤豆，就没有时间向天老爷汇报下面的灾难和不幸，以免天老爷听了发怒生气，再为难下面的平民百姓。青菜豆腐，是农家最家常不过的菜蔬了，但寓意不错。青菜是青，豆腐是白，二者烧在一起，意为一清二白，既表明主家吃饭的人是一清二白的，也表明了平民百姓的心愿：希望灶王爷推而广之，所有的官老爷都能做到一清二白，清正廉洁。

旧社会贪官污吏，天灾人祸，民不聊生。平民百姓只能把自己的心愿寄托在灶王爷身上。希望他们一年一度向天老爷"述职"时，多为平民百姓说说好话，多为平民百姓谋福利，保佑平民百姓平安无事，丰衣足食，安居乐业。但这样的愿望一直到中国共产党领导下的新中国才得以实现。特别是实行改革开放四十年来的今天，在以习近平同志为总书记的党中央正确领导下,大力发展经济,从严治党,严惩腐败,老虎苍蝇一起打,广大平民百姓有满满的获得感、幸福感和安全感,生活越来越好!

现如今,我们乡下人的生活也发生了巨变。住的平房大多变成了二层或三层的楼房,用稻草盖的平房已经绝迹。家里的炉灶也大多换成了液化气灶。但乡下人还是很善良,依然保留着祭灶的习俗。不过原先的内涵已不复存在,更多的是辞旧迎新的意思,为新的一年和更美好的新生活的到来祈福和祝愿!

祭灶图例/Stove sacrifice example

IV. Stove Sacrifice

After Laba (the 8th day in the last lunar month of a year), the New Year is getting closer and closer. Entering the 20th of the twelfth lunar month, it seems to be right at the foot of the New Year. On the 24th day of the month, almost every family in the countryside offers sacrifices to the stove, that is, to worship the Stove God (commonly known as the Stove Bodhisattva in my home village).

My countryside is located aside the lower reaches of the Yangtze River. The residents here are mainly from northern Jiangsu and Chongming Island, known respectively as "Jiangbei (north of Yangtze) people" and "Chongming people." Their dialects and lifestyles are integrated with each other. After more than a hundred years of getting along and living together, they have now formed the local population.

Every household here has a stove for cooking. The firewood is the stalks of rice, wheat, corn, soybeans, rapeseed, and other crops. The stove ash is then used to fertilize the fields, which finishes the cycle, very environmentally friendly. A custom here is that on the twenty-fourth day of the twelfth lunar month, every family must offer sacrifices to the Stove Bodhisattva. It seems that whether the family has provision of food and clothing totally relies on the blessing and gifts of their own Stove Bodhisattva.

The stove sacrifice ceremony is quite simple. For that day's dinner, every family will cook red bean rice. People here call it "the cooking of the 24th dinner." Every family has red beans grown and harvested by themselves. The vegetables are green vegetable (baby bok choy) and tofu. After the meal is served, the first bowl of red bean rice and the first bowl of green vegetables and tofu should be placed in front of the portrait of the Stove God on the stove, which will stay there until the Chinese New Year's Eve. There is also a pair of couplets posted on both sides of the portrait of the Bodhisattva. The left roll says, "To go up to heaven to report good things," and the right roll says, "To come down to the world to keep us safe." Two red candles are lit on the stove, and a handful of incenses are lit. The family kowtows and kneels to worship, which is not only to express gratitude to the Stove God for his protection in the past year, but also to pray for the coming year.

When I was a child, I just found it fun to watch the stove sacrifice without knowing why. It's interesting to reflect on it now. Why red bean rice? The older generation explained that when the Stove God is eating, he only focuses on counting the red beans in the bowl, so he has no time to report the disasters and misfortunes to the Lord of Heaven. Therefore, the latter would not get angry and give trouble to the common people below. Baby bok choy and tofu are the most common in the area, but they bear a good meaning. Bok choy is green, and tofu is white. The combination indicates clean and white. It not only shows that the people who eat the food are clear and clean but also expresses the wishes of the common people: We hope that the Stove God will extend the cleanness to everyone so that the officials can also be clean and honest.

In the old times, corrupt officials together with natural disasters made the common people live in dire straits. Average people can only pin their wishes on the Stove God. They hope that when he "reports" to the Lord of Heaven once a year, he will speak more nicely for the masses, work for their welfare, and bless them to be safe with enough food and clothing, and to live and work in peace and contentment. But such a wish was not realized until the new China under the leadership of the Communist Party. Especially today, after 40 years of reform and opening, under the correct leadership of the Party Central Committee with Comrade Xi Jinping as the general secretary, vigorously develop the economy, strictly govern the party, severely punish corruption, be they big as tigers or small as flies, the majority of ordinary people have a lot of feelings of achievements, happiness, and security. Our life is getting better and better.

Nowadays, the life of our rural people has also undergone tremendous changes. Most of the simple houses we lived in have become two- or three-story buildings, and the bungalows built with straw have disappeared. Most of the stoves at home have also been replaced with liquefied gas stoves. But the countryside people are still very kind and have retained the custom of offering sacrifices to stoves. However, the original connotation no longer exists, and it is more about saying goodbye to the old and welcoming the new, praying and wishing for the arrival of the new year and a better life.

图右：祭祀和烹饪用灶 / The stove used for cooking and sacrificing, to the right

五．桑家茶食

在上世纪三、四十年代，住在双桥镇附近十里八乡的人，只要一提起桑家茶食店，大家都会知道这个商店就在双桥镇；提起双桥镇，也都会想到这个镇上有个桑家茶食店，那就是当时当地小有名气的桑义隆茶食店。

我小时候也曾以为，桑家茶食店与双桥镇一定有着某种内在的联系。桑与双，读音相近，桑为sang，双为shuang，用当地崇明话来说，这两字都读作sang，这给人的印象是，双桥镇就该有个桑家，桑家就该住在双桥镇。

至于桑义隆茶食店是因何种原因和何时从镇江丹徒搬迁到双桥镇的，知情人都不在人世，也就无从知晓了。只知道桑家祖辈搬迁来双桥镇后，租用当地施家大地主在镇上十字街头的店铺，竖起了桑义隆茶食店的招牌，经营着自产自销茶食（糕点、糖果等）的生意。

茶食，主要是糕点等果品，是人们特别是老人、小孩常用的零食，更是过年过节人们人情往来相送的礼品，这在当时当地更是如此。

桑家茶食大致分为三大类，一是烘烤类，二是煎炸类，三是糖果类。这三大类食品，花色品种多种多样，在柜台的橱窗里摆放得琳琅满目，色香味齐全，引得路人垂涎三尺，踯躅不前，留连忘返。

烘烤类食品，主要有月饼、鸡蛋糕、老虎脚爪、脆饼、广东饼、桃酥、奶糕、云片糕、芝麻饼等。中秋时节，月饼是标志性的不可或缺的食品。桑家制作和销售的月饼，常见的品种有细沙、椒盐、伍仁、冬瓜月饼等等。在制作过程中，最复杂也最难做的就数冬瓜月饼了。冬瓜，是农家种植的最为普通的蔬菜，也是人们餐桌上最为普通的家常菜，种植简单方便，价格较为低廉。但要把冬瓜做成月饼馅，那可不那么容易和简单了。在制作中，难度最大的就是如何掌握冬瓜的水份。水份多了，就成不了馅，没法包进月饼中；水份过少，太干了，就成了冬瓜干，口感就差了。必须做到恰到好处。为此，负责制作茶食的桑家三儿子，人们常唤作"桑老三"，刻苦钻研，精心制作，带领两个徒弟，也是他自己的两个外甥，废寝忘食，边制作、边琢磨，才把桑家的冬瓜月饼做到了炉火纯青的境界，博得了众人的一致好评。就连当时镇上最刁钻刻薄的地主婆何佬佬也不得不承认"桑家的月饼还真是名不虚传！"

这里还有必要提一下奶糕，这是婴儿食品，为产妇们必不可少的有力帮手。奶糕的原料是大米粉和食糖。那时的婴儿在学会吃东西之前，除了吃奶，就是吃奶糕了。一次三至五片，开水调开，放在饭锅上蒸一下就可喂给婴儿吃了。这种食物很受产妇们的欢迎，婴儿也爱吃。

煎炸类食品有馓子、油绞绞、糖枣等。糖果类食品中，桑家很有名气的是寸金糖和冬瓜糖。制作寸金糖的工艺是非常烦琐和复杂的。熬制糖稀，然后反复揉搅，包裹酥芯，外黏芝麻，压挤成小手指粗细的条状，最后用小铡刀切成一寸长的样子，被称为寸金糖。这种糖入口即化，不黏牙齿，吃到嘴里，甜到心里，并且甜而不腻，味道悠长。我小时候就爱吃寸金糖，尽管七十年过去了，我至今还记忆犹新，似乎寸金糖的滋味还滞留在舌间和心里。

冬瓜糖的制作，其原理类似制作冬瓜月饼。但为何要用冬瓜来作原料这个问题，至今也是个谜。用现在的眼光来看，也许是和卫生、营养、健康、减肥等因素有关，也许是冬瓜这种食材价廉物美，还容易采购吧。

桑家茶食店的经营方针主要是自产自销，后来随着经营的发展和扩大，兼营批发业务。当时，南至薛季港、乐余镇，北至东界港（殷茅镇），西至十二圩港（三兴镇）、十一圩港和西界港，东至封头坝、六干河，这十里八乡的小商小贩都到桑家茶食店来批发茶食，如中秋时节的月饼，平时的馓子、油绞绞、脆饼、老虎脚爪、桃酥、奶糕、云片糕（当时这里被称作喜糕）等等。

桑家茶食的制作工艺不敢说有多精湛，但也有一定的规范和要领，不经过钻研和努力，也是难以掌握的，更何况还有祖传的秘方在里面，更是捉摸不透了。随着全面掌握桑家茶食工艺的桑老三的离世，很多的桑家茶食工艺也从此失传，不少茶食和糖果品种也因此淹没在历史的长河中。比如冬瓜月饼、寸金糖、冬瓜糖等，在市场上再也见不到了，就是在北京、上海、南京等大城市也找不到这种食品，就连名称也无人知晓。这真是太可惜，也太遗憾了。而流传至今的茶食就是较为普通也较为简单的煎馓子、贴脆饼了。人们提到的双桥镇脆饼的今生，那已是属于第三代传人了。通过上面的叙说，它的前生也就有点眉目了，其实那就是来自桑家，尤其是茶食大师桑老三流传下来的民间茶食手艺。

V. The Sang's Snacks

In the 1930s and 40s, mention Sang's snack store, people living nearby knew it was in Shuangqiao Town. And, mention the Shuangqiao Town, people knew there was a Sang's snack store. That was the pretty well-known Sang Yilong snack store.

I used to believe that there must be some connection between the store and the town. "Sang" and the Chinese word meaning double—"Shuang"—sound similar in Mandarin, and exactly the same in the local Chongming dialect. Therefore, my impression was that there must be a Sang household in Shuangqiao Town and that the Sangs got to live in Shuangqiao Town.

As to when and why Sang Yilong snack store moved from Dantu, Zhenjiang to Shuangqiao Town, those who knew all passed, so we wouldn't have any idea. What we do know is that after our ancestors moved to the town, they rented a store at a crossroads from the landlord Shi, erected a big sign and started a business of selling self-made desserts (cakes, candies, etc.).

Desserts, mainly cakes and candies, are a common snack, especially for the elderly and kids. It is also a decent gift on holidays, more so there at that time.

Sang's desserts usually fell in three categories: baked, deep fried, and candied. Various types of these three categories were placed dazzlingly in the windows. With the colors, aroma, and deliciousness, passers-by couldn't help drooling and wouldn't move further.

They baked mainly mooncakes, egg cakes, tiger paws, crispy pancakes, Guangdong pancakes, walnut crisps, milk cakes, layered cakes, and sesame cakes, etc. At the Mid-Autumn Festival, mooncakes are iconic and indispensable. Those made and sold by the Sangs were mostly stuffed either with bean paste, pepper and salt, five nuts, or winter melon. In the mooncakes, the most complicated and difficult to make should be the winter melon mooncake. Winter melon, a commonly grown vegetable in the countryside of southern China, is also a common dish. It's easy to grow and cheap to get. However, it's not easy or simple trying to make the melon into stuffing. The most difficult is the water in the melon. Too much water cannot form stuffing to be wrapped into the mooncake while too little makes it dry and taste bad. It must get to the "sweet" spot. For that purpose, the third son of the Sang's family, nicknamed Sang the Third and was responsible for the winter melon mooncake, studied it hard day and night with his two nephews, also his apprentices, and managed to make the winter melon mooncake perfect. It got unanimously praised by all who tried it. Even the meanest and cunniest wife of the landlord—He Laolao—had to admit that "Sang's mooncake's reputation is well-deserved!"

I have to shout out for the milk cake here which used to be a baby food and essential to new moms. Its ingredients are rice powder and sugar. Before babies learned to eat solid food, it was the second choice other than breast milk. Mix three to five slices of milk cake with hot water, steam, and voila! Mealtime for babies. This food was very welcome by new moms, as well as babies.

Deep fried food included Sanzi, twists, and date candy, etc. In candies, the well-known ones are the inch-gold candy and winter melon candy. The procedure for making inch-gold candy is very complicated—boiling sugar syrup, stirring, wrapping on the crispy core, sticking sesame outside, squeezing out long sticks the size of a pinky finger, and finally, cutting into an inch long, thus the name inch-gold candy. It melts in your mouth, never sticking to your teeth. Anyone who eats it can feel the heart being melted in the sweetness. The flavor, sweet but never too much, lasts long. I have loved the inch-gold candy since childhood. Seventy years passed, I still remember it in the bottom of my heart, as if the flavor has always been lingering on my tongue and in my mind.

The manufacturing of winter melon candy is similar to the winter melon mooncake. But it remains a mystery why winter melon was used as an ingredient. In today's standard, maybe winter melon is clean, nutritious, healthy, and helps lose weight, maybe also this melon is cheap and delicious and easy to get.

The business guideline of Sang's snack store was mainly self-made and self-sold. Later, with the development and enlargement of the business, they also did wholesale. At that time, customers from Xueji Harbor, Leyu Town to the south, East-Border Harbor (Yinmao Town) to the north, Twelfth Harbor (Sanxing Town), Eleventh Harbor, and West Border Harbor to the west, Fengtou Dam, Sixth Stem River to the east, as well as businessmen in the region all went to Sang's snack store to buy wholesale snacks, such as the mooncake at the Mid-Autumn Festival, and sanzi, twists, crispy pancakes, tiger paws, walnut crisps, milk cakes, layered cakes (called wedding cakes at that time), etc.

The craftsmanship of Sang's snacks, I dare not call it superb, but it required certain standards, specifications, and essentials. Without hard work and study, it's not easy to master, not to mention the ancestral recipe that makes it even harder to figure out. With the passing of Sang the Third, who comprehensively mastered Sang's craftsmanship, Sang's snack skills were lost in history, together with a lot of snack and candy varieties, such as the winter melon mooncake, inch-gold candy, and winter melon candy. They just disappeared from the market, not even available in big cities like Beijing, Shanghai, or Nanjing. Their names are also rarely known now. What a shame and pity! What has been passed down are the more common and simpler ones such as sanzi and crispy cakes. Today's crispy cakes survived in Shuangqiao Town is the third generation. The above narration tells the origin of the folk snack craftsmanship, which comes from the Sang's, especially from the master Sang the Third.

六．我们的外公外婆

说起我们的外公外婆，我们兄弟姐妹几个只有老大和老二见过外公，有一点点印象，但不深。其他人就没有这个福份了。至于外婆，亲外婆，谁也没有见过。我这里说的是一个真实的外婆，她给我们留下的印象终身难忘。

但是，说到这个外婆，必须首先要说说外公。因为没有外公，就没有这个外婆。从母亲断断续续的回忆里，我知道一些外公的情况。外公的命非常苦，中年丧妻（这是我们的亲外婆），自己还有工作，在一家地主的公司里做账房先生（就是现在的会计），晚上常常需要住在公司里。要照顾和带好自己只有十来岁的独生女（这就是我们的母亲），谈何容易。平时，他就把女儿托付给邻居照看。邻居姓朱，是个寡妇，也只有三十多岁，但生养了四个孩子（三男一女），大的只有十来岁，小的不过六七岁。其生活之艰难可想而知。当时，他们都居住在双桥镇南面的乡下。她替外公细心照料女儿，外公帮助她度过难关。一来二去，天长地久，二人情深意笃，重组新家庭。后来，他们搬迁到锦丰镇南面郁家桥乡下，因为外公在那边置办了房屋和地产。从此，外公的这位后妻就成了我们真实的外婆，她带来的孩子成了我们关系密切的舅舅和娘姨。郁家桥乡下的外婆家成了我们向往和每年必去的心中圣地，陪伴我们度过了欢乐和幸福的童年！

从我记事起，我见到的外公是长落面孔，剃的平头，面善话少。在外婆面前，他总是客客气气，言听计从的样子。背地里，外婆总称外公"老豆瓣"，口气虽是戏谑，但流露出来的是满满的亲昵。在我六、七岁即将上学的时候，外公问我的学名，我告诉了他，他听后高兴地笑着说："你有一个'堂'字，我也有个'堂'，我们都有一个'堂'……"此情此景，尽管过去了七十多年的时间，仍历历在目，记忆犹新。外公似乎觉得自己身上的某种东西在他的孙辈身上得到了体现，因而感到一丝兴奋和欣慰。（外公名字叫徐锦堂。）

非常不幸的是，就在解放前夕的一个早上，公司的几个员工把外公抬回了家。外公在睡梦中没有任何先兆，悄无声息地永远离开了外婆和我们。

当年外公同一个带有四个未成年孩子的女人结婚，不要说解放前，就是今天用世俗的眼光看来，也是不可思议的事情。有人会说他傻笨，有人会嘲笑他脑子进水，总之是不理解。然而外公不管他人说什么，勇敢地走自己的路。这体现了他的善良大度和聪明睿智。首先，他解决了自己的后顾之忧，工作之余有个温暖的家等着他；为女儿填补了一度失去的母爱，增添了兄弟姐妹情谊，有个较为长期的稳定的娘家。其次，外公也为寡母孤儿助了一臂之力，帮助他们买房置地，逐渐摆脱贫困，最后个个成家立业，结婚生子。这个外婆深明事理，其生养的四个子女也都有情有义。他们的大名，随的都是外公的"徐"姓，如果他们自己的老祖宗地下有知，一定会暗生妒意。在外公的丧礼上，三个舅舅都以其儿子的身份，为他披麻戴孝，送终，让他入土为安。

尽管外公离开了我们，但他用智慧和善举铺筑的娘家路一如既往地展现在母亲和我们的面前，始终没有中断过。我们每年较为固定的有两次去外婆家：一是过年时去拜年团聚；二是夏天（正值我们放暑假）去避暑消夏。新年里，且不说外婆家的好吃好喝、拿压岁钱等热闹气氛。给我印象最深的是，在外婆的房间里，飘散着浓浓的、香香的、甜甜的醪糟酒味，令人垂涎欲滴。这是外婆早为我们准备好的。这种味道伴随着我们成长，多少年过去了，似乎还在我们周围弥漫着。

炎热的夏季，午睡醒来，我总是喜欢跟在小娘舅的身后，到田里斩芦黍。他两手提着芦黍往回拖，叶子和田埂摩擦，发出"沙拉沙拉"的声音，我喜欢听这声音。在我听来，这声音就是一首欢快而热烈的田园丰收歌。

夜晚乘凉，又是我们小孩子高兴的时候。外婆的故事讲不完，我们也听不厌。邻近菜园子里织布娘娘的低声吟唱和筒管娘娘的引吭高歌，似乎在为外婆的故事伴奏，烘托气氛。她讲过一则尊老爱幼的感人故事《来郎吃的来郎肉》，说的是在那饥荒饿死人的年代，孙子来郎忍痛割肉让祖母充饥，而祖母不知情又省给孙子吃的事情。故事从何而来不得而知，或许纯属虚构，但外婆讲得真真切切，我至今还记得清清楚楚。

夜深了，在房间里躺在床上的时候，外婆依然非常兴奋，"丫头，我对你说，……"同母亲又聊起了家常。女人们的话题不外乎就是家长里短。外婆常常把一段时间以来儿子媳妇的事情讲给妈妈听，也免不了做些评述：谁精、谁好、谁懂事等等。母亲也把自己的委屈向外婆倾诉。因为母女也难得见面两人聊起来还没完没了。玉成弟给我补充了一个他所经历的事情。他说他那时候大概十二、三岁，有一次跟妈妈一起到外婆家。晚上三人就睡一个床，外婆妈妈两人睡一头，他睡另一头。在他印象中，那一个晚上，外婆妈妈一直聊天到天亮。两人不是亲生母女，胜似亲生母女。

外婆的两个特点对我的印象很深。一个是，她深受我国传统文化的影响，非常注重情面、熟谙人情世故。譬如说，我们晚辈攀亲来往，她一定关照要备厚礼，不能让人家看不起。一个是，她一辈子勤俭持家省吃俭用，她经常教育我们晚辈，说"铜钱银子连心肺"，一定要珍惜。

外婆始终信守和践行她对外公许下的照顾好其女儿的承诺，对我们母亲的生活时时牵挂于心，经常差遣舅舅们来看望。我父亲常年病患，外婆也心心挂念。那一年，父亲病故。按当地习俗，是玉成弟骑着自行车到外婆身边报丧。外婆后来几次提到，说看到还是十六、七岁的玉成可怜兮兮地跪在她面前的时候，她浑身顿时软了下来。尽管当时外婆年事已高，身体虚弱，但她还是不听子女劝阻，硬是坐着大舅舅的自行车后座，一、二十里土路，一路颠簸了近两个小时，前来悼念父亲，安慰母亲。在灵堂前，她声泪俱下，女婿长女婿短地哭诉，把现场的亲朋和乡邻感动得泪水涟涟。丈母娘哭女婿，难能可贵，后来很长一段时间在当地传为美谈。

岁月如梭也无情。娘家人中的长辈现在就只有阿姨健在。阿姨90多高龄，身体尚健。前两年我们去老家看望她，她还非常亲切地称呼我们的小名，拉着我们的手问长问短。其他的长辈都相继离我们而去，但我们后辈的情缘始终延续。就是在去年的一次聚会上，我们兄弟姐妹，以及舅舅阿姨家的同辈表亲，几乎全体到场，热闹非凡。大表弟大娘舅的儿子永华在那次聚会上感慨地说，"大娘舅不在了，我永华在！"言下之意，上一代的任务和使命已经完成了，下一代人一定会继续接过这段美好的缘分之棒，去谱写新的情缘。

多少年来，我们这一辈表亲关系始终非常的和谐融洽，虽然不在一地居住，但往来甚密，互通有无。时下，我们这一辈的大多数也都上了年纪，感叹命运的安排，更加珍惜亲情的缘分。我们还约定，以后每年会组织一次大聚会，精心维护由外公外婆为我们铺就的娘家路，使之坚固永远，日久弥新。

VI. Our Grandma and Grandpa

Concerning our maternal grandparents, among us siblings, only the two eldest have seen grandpa. They possess a vague impression of him. The others didn't have the blessing. As to Grandma, our biological one, nobody has ever seen her. The one I am talking about here is an authentic person, the Grandma who impressed us all our life.

But, before talking about this later Grandma, I have to introduce Grandpa first, because without him, there wouldn't have been this Grandma. From Mom's on and off recalling from her memories, I got to know something about Grandpa. His life was very hard, having lost his wife, our biological grandma, in his middle age. Grandpa had a job working as an accountant in a landowner's company and often had to spend nights there. It was easier said than done for him to take good care of his only daughter of around ten years old. The daughter later became our mom. Usually, he would entrust a neighbor to babysit her. The neighbor, surnamed Zhu, was a widow in her 30s. She herself had four kids, three boys and a girl, the eldest over ten and the youngest just about six or seven. Her life was understandably hard. At that time, they both resided in the countryside to the south of Shuangqiao Town. She took great care of Grandpa's daughter while Grandpa also helped her in her life. With time passing, the two developed deep feelings and love. They formed a new family. Later, they moved to the countryside of Yu's Bridge to the south of Jinfeng Town because Grandpa bought a house and real estate there. From then on, Grandpa's second wife became our real grandma, and her kids became our close uncles and aunts. Grandma's place at Yu's Bridge became our pilgrimage of yearning, desire, and a yearly must-visit. How it formed our happy childhood!

From my earliest recollections, what I saw about Grandpa was a long face, crew-cut hair, and kind expressions with few words. In front of Grandma, he was always polite and gentle. Behind him, Grandma always referred to him as "Old Man" with a joking tone, which, however, exposed their full intimacy.

When I was about to go to school around six or seven years old, Grandpa asked me about my school/official name. After hearing my answer, he smiled delightfully, "There's a 'Tang' in your name, and one in mine too. We share the 'Tang.'..." That moment was carved in my memory. Although having occurred more than 70 years ago, it is fresh as yesterday. Grandpa seemed to feel that something in him was represented in his grandkids, therefore, he was excited and satisfied (Grandpa's name was Xu Jintang).

Very unfortunately, on a morning right before the liberation of China, several of his coworkers carried him back on a stretcher. He quietly left Grandma and us in his sleep without any sign.

That Grandpa married a woman with four young kids was incredible, even by today's social standards, not to mention before the liberation. Some would think he was foolish; others would mock his "stupidity," etc. They wouldn't understand him. However, Grandpa bravely walked his own path, disregarding what others said. That reflected his kindness, generosity, and wisdom. First of all, he solved his own worries and had a warm home waiting for him after work; he also found a mom and siblings for his daughter, so that she had a steady mom at home. Second, Grandpa also helped the single mom with her kids. He helped them buy houses and land, rid their poverty, and finally get married and have their own families. Grandma knew better and her children were also affectionate. Their names all followed Grandpa's surname, "Xu." If their own ancestors were aware under the ground, they would be jealous. At Grandpa's funeral, my three uncles put on the mourning clothes and did filial piety as his sons in order for him to rest in peace.

Although Grandpa left us, his tradition of going home to see Grandma, built with his wisdom and charity, spread in front of mom and us as always, never pausing. We had two fixed occasions to visit Grandma: one was during the Chinese New Year; the other was summer vacation. In the New Year, other than the good eating, drinking, and red envelope money, etc., what impressed me most was in Grandma's room, there was the thick and sweet aroma of rice wine that made us drool. That was what Grandma made before we came to visit. This aroma accompanied our childhood. Decades have passed, but it seems to still be around us.

During hot summer at Grandma's home, after the noon nap, I would follow my youngest uncle to go to the field to cut sweet canes. When he dragged them back, the rumbling sound from the friction of the leaves with the field ridge was my favorite. To me, the sound was a happy and enthusiastic harvest song.

The evening's cooling-taking[1] was another fun time for us kids. Grandma's stories never ended and we were never tired of listening to them. In the neighboring vegetable gardens, grasshoppers were singing in a low voice and katydids in high, which seemed to be creating the atmosphere for Grandma's story telling. She once told a moving story called "Lai Lang Eats Lai Lang's Flesh," about how in the famine era, a grandson suffered great pain to cut his flesh for his grandma to eat while his grandma, unaware of the origin of the meat, instead, saved it for him. Nobody knows where the story comes from. It might as well be fiction. However, Grandma told it as if it were true, which is still clear in my mind.

In the deep night, Grandma was still quite awake in her bed. "My girl, let me tell you...," she was chatting with my mom. Women usually talk about other families and households. Grandma used to tell mom about her sons and daughters-in-law, together with her comments about who was smarter, who was better, and who was more sensitive, etc. Mom also told Grandma about her life. Their conversations seemed to last forever as they rarely saw each other. My brother Yucheng told me what he experienced. He said he was about 12 or 13 years old when he once went to Grandma's home with mom. At night, they slept on one bed. Grandma and Mom on one side and he on the other. In his memory, that night, Grandma and Mom chatted until daylight. They were not biologically related but seemed more intimate than that.

Grandma impressed me in two ways. One was that she was deeply influenced by our traditional culture and therefore

---

1 Cool-taking: in the summer evening when the heat starts to cool down, people get to the outside to enjoy the coolness while chatting, telling stories, or just relaxing.

attached importance to face and social sophistication. For example, when we went to visit our relatives, she would advise that we prepare significant gifts so we wouldn't be looked down upon. The other was that she was economical all her life. She often told us that money is connected with our heart and lungs and should be cherished.

Grandma always believed and practiced her commitment for Grandpa to take good care of his daughter. She was always concerned with my mom's life and often asked my uncles to come visit us. My father was sick for years, which was also Grandma's concern. When he passed, my brother rode a bike to Grandma's home to inform the obituary. Later, Grandma talked about it on several occasions. She said when she saw my 16-year-old brother kneel in front of her miserably, she almost collapsed right away. Although she was quite old and weak and despite her kids trying to dissuade her, she insisted on sitting on the back of my uncle's bike for about two hours on the bumpy dirt road to come to mourn my father and console my mom. In front of the mourning hall, she wept and cried for her son-in-law, which moved the relatives and neighbors on the spot to tears. Mother-in-law mourning for son-in-law is precious. That story spread locally for a long time as a treasure.

Time flies mercilessly. Now my older generation is all gone except my aunt. She is in her 90s, still quite healthy. A couple of years ago we went to our home village to see her. Still addressing us with our nicknames, she held our hands and asked about us. The others in the older generation are gone, but our later generations' relations continue as always. At a reunion last year, my siblings and cousins from my uncles and aunts almost all showed up, extraordinarily lively. My eldest cousin, from my eldest uncle, said emotionally there, "Your eldest uncle passed, but I, Yonghua, am still here!" He was conveying that the older generation had done their mission, and the next generation will relay this beautiful relationship to write a new chapter.

For many years, my generation has been getting along with our cousins. Although we don't live in the same city, we often visit each other. Presently, most of us are getting old. While we sighed at fate's arrangements, we cherish more our relationship. We have decided that we shall have a big reunion every year to carefully maintain the Home Road built by Grandma and Grandpa. We shall make it newer each day and sturdy forever.

小镇一角/A corner in town

七．女性前辈

我这里要说的桑家两位女性前辈，如今见过的人已很少了，知道的恐怕也不多。她们虽离开我们半个多世纪了，但她们的音容笑貌还时不时地在我的脑海中浮现。她们是母女俩，一个是我的奶奶（祖母），一个是我的姑姑（我们叫她大伯）。

我的奶奶，用现在的话说，可算是个女强人。那时候，桑家从镇江丹徒搬迁到双桥镇后，奶奶支撑着一个大家庭，支撑着桑义隆茶食店。尽管期间经过两次大劫难[1]，但结果家没有散掉，店也没有垮掉，这就是奇迹。尤其是在旧社会。

奶奶育有三儿一女。在双桥镇定居后，老大一家分开居住，另立门户。老二、老三和女儿三家居住在一起，生活在一起，当地称为"共家"。能把三家大大小小十多口人拢在一起，同吃同住同生活，并做到相安无事，这本身就说明，奶奶确有过人之处，能干、有本事、有魄力。

尤其是要说一说我姑姑的情况。姑姑当时早已婚嫁，而且也有二子，为什么还挤在这个大家庭里的呢？

当初全家从镇江来到双桥镇的时候，姑父似乎老不情愿，看不上这个小地方，死活要去上海闯荡。他不听劝阻，不管不顾妻子和两个年仅十岁左右的儿子，一走了之，并且十多年杳无音讯。

被丢下的我的姑姑和两个表哥怎么办？住哪里？怎么过日子？

乡下有个传统，说"嫁出去的女儿泼出去的水"，娘家是可以不闻不问的。家里也有人受这种传统观念的影响，表露出了这个倾向。据说，奶奶听到后非常气愤，甚至拍桌子大骂："这是什么混账话！轻飘飘一句泼出去的水，我十月怀胎容易吗？我女儿，过去是、现在是、将来也永远是我身上掉下来的一块肉！你们心不疼，我心疼！"看着满脸愁容的女儿和依偎在其身旁的两个外孙，奶奶心碎了，眼泪顿时流了下来。她当即拍板，把女儿一家三口拢在自己的卵翼之下。

而姑姑又是另一种心态，尽管是自己的娘家，但毕竟也受到那种传统观念的影响，总有一种寄人篱下的感觉。时时处处、一言一行都得看人脸色，小心翼翼，谨小慎微，不敢多说一句

---

[1] "两次大劫难"指的是抗日战争中奶奶的二儿子被土匪绑票，以及解放前国民党部队撤退时把小镇洗劫一空。

话，不敢多走一步路。姑姑常常起早贪黑，外出帮人家做鞋帽、缝衣服，把所挣来的钱交给她妈妈。两个儿子也非常懂事，不是扫地烧火，就是挑水洗碗，后来还跟着他们的舅舅学做茶点，掌握了制作茶点、糖果的手艺，为他们今后的生活和工作打好了坚实的基础。

姑姑他们在大家庭共同生活了十年左右，直到解放，并在土改后分得了房屋和土地，才搬离出去独户生活。后来，两个表哥都成了供销社的职工，并先后结婚成家，过着丰衣足食的生活，大表哥后来还做了乡供销社的经理。

上世纪50年代初，新政权成立不久，上海公安部门通过这里的乡政府，找到我姑姑来了。原来，失联十多年的姑父据说是因为吸毒还是因为其他什么原因被劳教，释放后的去向成了问题。他没有其他亲人，只有姑姑他们是他首选的、唯一的亲人。姑父应该是提出了这个意向，政府部门就来做姑姑的工作了。

提起姑父，姑姑气不打一处来。十多年了，还以为这个人早在地球上消失了。十多年的积怨，十多年的艰辛，向谁倾诉，用多少时间也倾诉不完。拒绝他，也顺理成章，完全在理上。但是拒绝的话，他就走投无路，只得继续在社会上浪荡。但他毕竟是两个孩子的父亲，这个亲情还是割不断的。接纳他吧，虽然心里肯定有疙瘩，但也算是圆了他们父子团聚的梦。不管怎么样，他最终还是知道这里是他的家，是他的归宿。原谅他，就当他是"浪子回头"吧。于是，姑父终于回家了，带着沉重的歉疚和懊悔回家了。

后来的日子算是平静。姑父做起了他的茶食生意以谋生机，家庭和和睦睦，老两口也相敬如初。姑姑后来得了恶病卧床不起的日日夜夜，姑父始终陪伴左右，精心服侍，不怕脏，不怕臭，不厌其烦地换纱布、换药、倒屎倒尿，也算尽到了作为丈夫的责任。

奶奶和姑姑的故事很多，这里记述的仅仅是一些梗概。从我们桑家两位女性前辈的身上，我看到了善良的心地、宽广的胸怀、为人的美德。

VII. Stories of Two Female Ancestors

The two female ancestors of our Sang family are not known by many current people, let alone seen. They have been away from us for more than half a century, but their images and voices still merge sometimes in my mind. They were mother and daughter, one being my grandma on my father's side, and the other my aunt who we called Big Aunt.

My grandma could be considered, to use the modern word, a tough woman. At that time, after the Sang family moved from Dantu, Zhenjiang to Shuangqiao Town, she supported the whole family, holding up the business of Sang Yilong snack store. In spite of the two big disasters[1], the family survived together with their store.

My grandma had three sons and a daughter. After settling down in Shuangqiao Town, the eldest lived separately in his own household. The other three lived together, locally called "Co-family." More than ten people, old and young, lived together, ate together, keeping harmony, which indicated that Grandma was outstanding. She was capable, able, and courageous.

I especially wanted to talk about my aunt. She had long been married with two sons. Why would she stay in this big family?

When the whole family moved from Zhenjiang to Shuangqiao Town, her husband was very reluctant. He looked down upon this little town and was determined to go to Shanghai to explore. He didn't listen to dissuasion and left his wife and two roughly ten-year-old sons, without any word for more than 10 years.

What should my abandoned aunt and two cousins do? Where should they live? How do they support themselves?

In China, there's a tradition called "married daughters are like water thrown out." Their original families didn't have to help the daughters after their marriage. Some people in my family were also influenced by this concept and expressed it to

---
[1] The two big disasters refer to the kidnapping of my grandmother's second son by bandits during the Anti-Japanese War, and the looting of the town by the retreating Kuomintang troops right before liberation.

Grandma. It's said that Grandma was very angry hearing this, even cursing and slapping the table, "What kind of BS is that? A single light phrase of throwing out water! Was it easy that I was pregnant with her in the months? My daughter used to be, is now, and will always be part of my flesh! You guys don't care. I do!" Looking at her worried daughter and two grandsons clinging to her side, Grandma's heart broke. Her tears streamed down her cheeks. She decided right there and was determined to take her daughter's family under her wings.

However, my aunt held another mentality. Although it was her own parents' home, affected by the traditional concept, she always felt like a guest. Everywhere, every move and word from her was cautious. She didn't dare to say one more word or move one step further if not necessary. She got up early and went to bed late, going out to make shoes and clothes for people and gave the money to her mom. Her two sons were very sensible as well. They helped with the house doing chores—cleaning, tending the cooking fire, or washing the dishes. Later, they learned from their uncle how to bake and grasped the skills of making snacks and candy. This made a solid foundation for their future life and work.

My aunt lived with the big family for about 10 years until the liberation when she was assigned a house and some land. Later, my two cousins became staff in the supply store and got married, living an abundant life. The elder one later worked as the manager of the store.

In the early 1950s, soon after the new regime was established, the Shanghai Public Security came to look for my aunt through the local government. It turned out that my uncle who lost contact with us was put into prison for taking drugs or something. Nobody knew where he should go now that he was released. He didn't have other family, my aunt being his priority and only family. He probably proposed this and the government came to talk with my aunt.

My aunt was very mad at my uncle. A decade went by, she had thought that he had disappeared from this planet. All the grudges, all the hardships, who could she have told? It'd take forever to pour them all. It was totally reasonable and moral to turn him down. However, he, after all, was the father of her two kids. The relation was always there. Accepting him, although feeling a grudge in the heart, would be realizing the dream of reuniting father and son. Anyway, he had realized this was his home, his returning place. My aunt decided to forgive him as if taking him as a returning prodigal. Therefore, my uncle came back home finally, with heavy guilt and regret.

The later days were quite peaceful. My uncle started his business of making snacks to earn a living. The family was harmonious, and the couple were back to the good old days. My aunt later got a severe disease and had to stay in bed day and night. My uncle accompanied her all the time, taking care of her diligently. Without any complaint, he patiently changed her gauze, dumped her toilet stuff, and applied medicine, which fulfilled his responsibilities as her husband.

There are a lot of stories about my grandma and aunt. Here I just recorded some basics. From our ancestors, I saw kindness, open-mindedness, and morality.

西桥/The West Bridge

八．锦文哥

双桥镇西桥头的沿街十字路口，开着一家裁缝店。双桥镇几经变迁，裁缝店依然是裁缝店，什么时候开张的，什么时候关闭的，唯有老双桥镇人才略有所知。

店主是我的锦文哥，准确地说，是我的堂姐夫。我这位堂姐，在我这一辈里排行老大。长者为大，我们都很尊敬大姐和大姐夫。从我小时候记事起，就知道有一位做裁缝的哥哥。在我印象中，他总是那么的和蔼可亲，成天笑眯眯的。我每次见到他，都有一种亲切温馨的感觉，并亲热地用带着点苏北口音的腔调叫他一声"哥哥"。这似乎成了习惯，一直延续了下来。

据说，锦文哥十四、五岁就身背行囊，只身从苏北来到江南这个小镇双桥镇谋生。从学手艺开始，然后自立开店，服务于周边的百姓。当时，这里的人们穿的衣服没有现成的可买，大多自己到布店买布料，然后请专门的裁缝师傅手工制作。多年来，锦文哥靠自己的精湛手艺和诚信人品，赢得了小镇居民和邻近村民们的信赖，生意越做越红火，天天起早贪黑忙个不停。

锦文哥的裁缝手艺可谓了得。我印象中，只要是他熟悉并且见过的人，说去请他做件什么衣服裤子的，如果你不那么特别讲究，他可以不用"量体"即可"裁衣"的。通常是这样，哪位去他裁缝店，拿了一块布料说要做件衣服，他上下打量一番，说好了，过几天来拿就是。然后过几天去取衣服，他还会说你试试。试了之后肯定合身，皆大欢喜。

锦文哥不仅手拿针线是行家，年轻力壮时，挑起扁担也是一把好手。土改后，家里分到了土地，农忙时节，他就下地干活，不是挑泥，就是拉粪、挑粮、担水，一样不差。

在那普遍贫穷的时代，尽管锦文哥的生意不错，但是靠这种苦力营生，也着实不大容易。"新三年旧三年，缝缝补补再三年"，这是大多普通百姓的着衣原则。顾客带上布料到缝纫店制衣，算是家境富足的。对于锦文哥来说，省时省力，也能多挣几个钱。但方圆几里有钱人家寥寥可数，较少有这样的生意。大多的情况是，左右相邻一合计，各自买上布料，请师傅上门服务，按天计费，这样就来得划算。我印象中，那个时候裁缝师傅上门一天服务，收费标准1.2至1.5元不等。对于这样的生意，锦文哥从不推却，但这样的话可累坏了锦文哥。因为他只有一台缝纫机，通常是白天扛着缝纫机出去吃百家饭，忙碌一天之后，又把缝纫机扛回店里，晚上还得加班做些零星活。为生计，为了要养活上有老下有小的一大家子，日复一日，年复一年。做衣服、种地、扛缝纫机、挑担，日积月累，锦文哥的右肩上还生出了一个小馒头似的肉包。这是锦文哥辛勤劳动的印记，更像是一枚不朽的奖章。

锦文哥是如何成为我的堂姐夫的呢？说起来也是一段佳话。那时候，锦文哥应约到我大伯父家做裁缝活的时候，意想不到的好事来了。他在裁剪缝纫，大堂姐坐着一边看，看着锦文哥娴熟的手艺活，非常入神，一坐就是几个小时。她还不断地给师傅递剪刀送尺子，穿个针引条线，似以徒弟的身份忙前忙后，后来也就慢慢成了师傅的得力助手。从此后，两人形影不离，相互之间萌生了爱慕之情。值得庆幸和称道的是，我大伯父大伯母同意了这门喜事。老俩口非常看好锦文哥的人品和技艺，真是看在眼里喜在心头。这桩自由恋爱的婚姻，在当时的这个小镇上还是罕见的，并且结局是如此的圆满和美好，因此在全镇传为美谈。不仅如此，还拨动了不少姐妹们沉寂的心灵。

在过去一度艰难的日子里，我们家给哥哥姐姐家增添了不少麻烦，他们也都给了我们很大的帮助。我们去做衣服，哥哥不仅分文不取，免费给我们增添布料，还为我们烧菜做饭。我本人结婚时，锦文哥专门给我做了一件呢子婚服，既光彩又喜气。我们每次去看望他们，哥哥姐姐总是好吃好喝的热情招待。哥哥一句"弟子来了……"直暖人心。吃饭的时候，锦文哥不是夹菜就是添饭，他一直担心我们拘束不敢多吃，经常悄悄地盛满一碗饭，出其不意地倒入我们的饭碗里。饭后，锦文哥马上准备好热水毛巾让我们"洗把脸"。最后，又给我们带上好吃的回家。

锦文哥虽然离开我们十多年了，他的裁缝店现在也不见了踪影，但他在裁缝店忙碌时的娴熟动作和音容笑貌时不时地浮现在眼前，令人铭记心中，终生难忘。

VIII. Brother Jinwen

At the crossroads of the West Bridge in Shuangqiao Town, there was a tailor shop. The town had gone through many changes, but the tailor shop was still there. When it was open or closed, only the old locals knew something about it.

The store owner was my Brother Jinwen, to be more precise, my cousin-in-law Wang. His wife, my cousin, was the eldest in our generation. Therefore, we respected our eldest cousin and cousin-in-law. For as long as I can remember, I have always known this tailor brother. In my memory, he was always kind and amiable, smiling all the time. Every time I saw him, I felt warm and cordial. I would address him "Elder Brother" with a bit of Northern Jiangsu accent. That habit stuck for the rest of time.

It was said that at 14 or 15 years old, Brother Jinwen carried his luggage to Shuangqiao Town from Northern Jiangsu, trying to make a living. He started as an apprentice, then opened his own shop to serve nearby people. At that time, there were no ready-to-go clothes available for purchase. Most people went to the cloth store to buy cloth before going to a tailor for making clothes. Through his years' of fine expertise and honesty, Brother Jinwen won the trust of the residents and the nearby countrymen. His business was prosperous and he worked day and night.

Brother Jinwen's craftsmanship could be considered as excellent. In my impression, as long as the customer was familiar to him, and was not peculiar about their clothes, he could make clothes for them without even measuring. It was generally like this: you would go to his shop with a piece of cloth telling him what you want, he would look at you up and down before telling you to pick it up in a couple of days. Then when the time came, you would go to pick it up. He would want you to try it on. It would be guaranteed that it would fit you. So, everybody would be happy.

Brother Jinwen was not only good at threads and needles, but he was also good at carrying stuff on poles. After the Land Reform, he was assigned some land. During farming times, he would work in the fields, carrying mud, manure, grains, and water, all in his control.

During that universally impoverished time, although Brother Jinwen had a good business, it was not easy to earn living with this hard work. "Three years of new, three years of old, and three years of mending" was the clothing principle for most common people. Customers bringing cloth to a tailor shop were kind of rich. To Brother Jinwen, that saved time and labor and could make him more money. However, there were few such businesses as there were few rich people around. The more common thing was, some neighbors would work together, buying some cloth to ask the tailor to work in their home. The daily payment was more worthwhile. To my recollection, tailors charged 1.2 to 1.5 yuan per day if they were asked to work in the client's home. Brother Jinwen never rejected such small deals; however, it was grueling work. As he had only one sewing machine, he usually carried his machine out to work in people's households in the daytime and carried it back to the store to work more at night, for living, for supporting his family, day after day and year after year. Making clothes, farming, carrying the sewing machine, and carrying stuff with the pole, Brother Jinwen's right shoulder developed a swollen bun. It was a mark showing his hard work, but more like an immortal medal.

How did Brother Jinwen become my cousin's husband? This is a good story. Once, when he was invited home to work for my uncle, unexpected romance started. While he was there cutting and sewing, my cousin would sit there watching his skillful craftsmanship, totally mesmerized, for hours and hours. She would also help pass scissors or ruler, thread the needle, etc., like an apprentice. She later became a great help to the tailor. Afterwards, the two were inseparable. Love grew. Luckily, my uncle and aunt agreed to their relationship. They liked Brother Jinwen's character and crafts from the bottom of their hearts. This free love was rare in the town at that time. With such a beautiful ending, the story was spread as a great romance. Not only that, but it also touched many girls' quiet minds.

During the difficult days, my family bothered his family a lot, the latter offering tremendous help. When we went to get our clothes made, Brother not only did so for free, but also added cloth and cooked for us. When I myself got married, Brother Jinwen made a woolen wedding gown for me, making me look brilliant and nice. Every time we went to visit them, they always entertained us with good things to eat and drink. Brother's remark, "Here's my younger brother...," warmed my heart. During the meal, he would help us with the dishes and rice. He was worried that we were shy and wouldn't eat enough. Therefore, he would prepare an extra bowl of rice and unexpectedly pour it into our bowls. After eating, he would provide hot water and a towel for us to refresh ourselves. Finally, when we left his home, he would give us more nice food to take home.

Although Brother Jinwen has been away from us for more than a decade and his tailor shop has been out also, his skill in making clothes and his sweet smiles merge in front of my eyes more often than not. I will never forget that.

记忆中的小镇一角/A corner of the town in memory

九．镇上女孩

所谓"那时候"，指的是解放前后那段时间，正当新旧社会、新旧思想、新旧观念等等交替之际。人们的思想观念，如在婚姻问题上，表现得纷繁复杂，多种多样。这种现象，在双桥镇，相比临近的乡村，体现地更为明显和突出。

俗话说：男大当婚，女大当嫁。现就后一句而言，镇上当嫁的女孩儿不少，她们的心思不要猜，也猜不透，但从她们的行动上可以看出端倪，略知一二。

有人说双桥镇这个由长江滩涂围垦出来的小集镇，风水好，是块宝地，出人才，更出美女。镇上的女孩儿个个出落得亭亭玉立、婀娜多姿，既有娇美的容貌，又有修长的身姿，且都聪明能干。娟姐就是其中佼佼者之一。她是我堂姐，人如其名，娟秀俊美，平时寡言少语，文文静静。当她认识、了解了裁缝王师傅后，就心动了，萌生了爱慕之情。她看中的不仅是王师傅的精湛手艺，更是他的人品和为人，诚实善良，和蔼可亲，还没有任何如抽烟、喝酒等不良嗜好。如此品行，在解放前的旧社会实属难得。好在我的大伯父、大伯母非常开通，尊重女儿的心愿，同意了这门亲事。这段自由恋爱的姻缘在小镇被传为佳话，也给全镇小姐妹们带来了福音，树立了榜样。

双桥镇西街的十字路口，有家鞋店，店主大家称他为冯皮匠。他人高马大，生养的两个女儿也是高挑身材，漂漂亮亮，且都到了当嫁的年纪。大女儿早已订有娃娃亲，婆家在南通。当时，男方携带聘金和彩礼前来催婚。冯皮匠高兴地一口答应下来，并选好了日子。但大女儿一开始就不同意这门亲事，她从来没有见过这个男人，更谈不上了解了。于是，哭着闹着，死也不愿意。眼看离办事的日子越来越近，父母急得团团转，对大女儿不是哄，就是骂，甚至动手打，也无济于事。小女儿把这一切都看在眼里，心里也不好受：既同情父母的难处，又理解姐姐的执着。于是，她自告奋勇，愿意代替姐姐成全这门亲事，最终解决了冯家的一大难题。大女儿无奈之中离家出走，参加了革命工作，据说后来还担任了苏北某地妇联的领导干部。至于她妹妹对自己的终身大事是怎么想的，怀着什么样的心思，那就不得而知，猜也猜不出来了。

住在我大伯父家斜对门的兰姐，长得不错，但就是生性泼辣，敢说敢做，说话做事干脆利落。对自己的个人问题她早就有言在先：自己的事情自己解决，不需要爷娘操心。当时，国民党军队有一个连驻扎在镇上。一天，一个士兵对兰姐非礼。兰姐不仅当场把他臭骂了一顿，还径直闯进连部，对连长连珠炮似地状告那位士兵的劣行。这位知识分子出身的连长，不再像平时板着个脸，而是始终微笑着盯着兰姐看，仔细听着兰姐的申诉，后来把那个士兵关了禁闭。兰姐虽然平时见过这位连长，但没有像这次这么近距离地看他，心里突然有了一种异样的感觉。不打不相识。打这以后，兰姐有事没事就往连部跑，士兵们都以礼相待，甚至有些敬畏之感。一天晚上，连长同兰姐密谈了几个小时。据兰姐后来透露，这位连长认清形势，决定找机会弃暗投明，解甲归田，同兰姐结婚。不久，他果然带着部队向解放军投诚，他被获准回到小镇，践行了自己的诺言。

事后表明，兰姐没有找错对象。这位连长姓周，南京人氏。婚后他勤勤恳恳，任劳任怨，不怕苦不怕累，重活脏活抢着干。他后来还把在南京的老娘接了过来，一家人过着和睦、安稳、幸福的生活。他每次遇见我，总是笑脸相迎，用带着浓重的南京口音嘘寒问暖，亲热得很。遗憾的是，他在文革中受到了冲击，即使他拿出有叶飞将军签字的投诚证明也没有用。

在自主找对象方面，我二堂姐贞姐要幸运得多！小镇解放了，不久开展了轰轰烈烈的土地改革运动。斗地主，分田地，一片热闹繁忙的景象！那时候经常召开群众大会，主持会议的通常是土改工作队的王同志。他那带有常熟口音的讲话，铿锵有力，爱憎分明，有很大的吸引力和号召力，经常被台下群众的鼓掌声和口号声打断。贞姐被他的魅力所打动，每次开会她都尽量挤在前面，目不转睛地看着他，听他讲话。通过家访（到家中了解疾苦…），王同志也认识和了解贞姐，被贞姐的热情善良、美丽大方所吸引。两人逐渐从相识到相知，从相知到相爱，最后终成眷属。后来贞姐跟随他到常熟工作，日子过得美满幸福。

双桥镇是个小镇，人口不多，但女孩子们向往和追求婚姻自由的例子却不少。还比如小镇南市梢施家三姐，为了寻求心仪之人，一直等到三十多岁成了"老丫头"，才终于遂愿，同崇实中学的张先生结为伉俪。岁月如梭。当时这些妙龄少女如今都已垂垂老矣，也许有的已不在人世，但她们当时追求婚姻自由的勇气永远留在后一辈人的心中，并广为传颂。

IX. The Girls in the Town

At that time refers to the period right before and after liberation, when the old and new societies, old and new ideas, old and new concepts, etc. were transitioning. People's ideas, such as those on marriage issues, were complicated and varied. This phenomenon was more obvious and prominent in Shuangqiao than in the neighboring villages.

As the saying goes: people should get married when they are old enough. Now, as for the girls, there were many in the town who were at that age. Don't try to guess what they were thinking; you couldn't guess even if you tried, but you can know a little bit by observing their actions.

Some people say that Shuangqiao, a small market town reclaimed from the Yangtze River beach, has good feng shui and is a treasure land that produces talents and beauties. All the girls in the town were graceful and elegant, with beautiful looks and slender figures, and they were all smart and capable. Sister Juan was one of the best. She is my cousin, as her name suggests, beautiful and pretty, usually taciturn and quiet. When she met and knew more about Mr. Wang, the tailor, her heart was moved, and she fell in love with him. She was attracted not only by Wang's exquisite craftsmanship, but also by his character and personality. He was honest, kind, amiable, and had no such bad habits as smoking or drinking. Such character was rare in the old society before liberation. Fortunately, my uncle and aunt, very open-minded, respected their daughter's wishes and agreed to this marriage. This free love marriage has become a legend in the town, and it has also brought good news to the younger girls in the town and set an example.

At the intersection of West Street in Shuangqiao Town, there was a shoe store. The owner Mr. Feng was tall and strong, and his two daughters were also tall and pretty, and both were of marriageable age. The elder daughter had already been engaged to a guy in Nantong when she was a little girl. So, this day, the man came with betrothal money and gifts to urge the marriage. Mr. Feng happily agreed and chose a date, but the elder daughter had not agreed to the marriage from the beginning. She had never seen this man, let alone knew him. So, she cried and made a fuss, saying she would rather die. As the wedding date approached, the parents were anxious. It was no use that they coaxed or scolded the daughter or even beat her. The younger daughter saw all this and felt bad: she sympathized with her parents' difficulties and understood her sister's persistence. To everyone's astonishment, she volunteered to help her sister complete the marriage and finally solved this major problem for the Feng family. The elder daughter ran away from home in desperation and joined the revolution. It is said that she later served as a leading cadre of the Women's Federation in northern Jiangsu. As for what her younger sister thought about her marriage and what she had in mind, it is unknown to us and there is no way to guess.

Sister Lan, who lived caddy-corner from my uncle's house, was good-looking, but she was a hot-tempered person. She dared to speak and act and was decisive in her words and deeds. She had long made it clear that she would decide her marriage by herself, and her parents didn't need to worry about it. At that time, a company of the Kuomintang army was stationed in the town. One day, a soldier harrassed Sister Lan, who not only scolded him on the spot, but also rushed into the company headquarters and complained to the company commander about the soldier's misdeeds. The company commander, who was an intellectual, didn't hold a stern face as usual, but kept smiling at Sister Lan, listening carefully to her complaints, and later put the soldier in solitary confinement. Although Sister Lan had seen this company commander before, she had never seen him as close as this time, and she suddenly had a strange feeling in her heart. No fight, no acquaintance. After that, Sister Lan would go to the company headquarters whether she had something to do or not, and the soldiers treated her with courtesy, even respect. One night, the company commander had a secret conversation with Sister Lan for several hours. According to Sister Lan, he recognized the situation and decided to turn over a new leaf by retiring from the army and marrying

Sister Lan. Soon, he surrendered to the People's Liberation Army with his troops. He was allowed to return to the town and fulfill his promise.

It turned out that Sister Lan had not chosen the wrong guy. The company commander, surnamed Zhou, was from Nanjing. After getting married, he was diligent and hardworking, not afraid of hardship and fatigue, and rushed to do heavy and dirty work. Later, he brought his mother from Nanjing to live with them. The family lived a harmonious, stable, and happy life. Every time he met me, he always greeted me with a smile affectionately, asking me about my well-being with a strong Nanjing accent. Unfortunately, he was affected during the Cultural Revolution, and was helpless even if he produced the Certificate of Surrender signed by General Ye Fei.

In terms of finding a partner on her own, my second cousin Sister Zhen seemed much luckier! The town was liberated, and soon a vigorous land reform movement was launched with fighting against landlords and reassigning lands. What a lively and busy scene! At that time, mass meetings were often held, and the person who presided over the meetings was usually Comrade Wang from the land reform work team. His speech with a Changshu accent was sonorous and powerful, showing clearly what he liked and what he hated, which had great attraction and appeal, and was often interrupted by the applause and slogans of the masses below the stage. Sister Zhen was moved by his charm. Every time she attended such a meeting, she tried to squeeze to the front, staring at him and listening to him speak. Through home visits (going to the family to understand the sufferings ...), Comrade Wang also knew and understood Sister Zhen, and was attracted by her enthusiasm, kindness, beauty, and decency. The two gradually went from acquaintance to understanding, from understanding to love, and finally became a couple. Later, Sister Zhen followed him to work in Changshu, and they lived a happy life.

Shuangqiao Town is a small town with a small population, but there are many examples of girls yearning for and pursuing freedom of marriage. For example, the third sister of the Shao's family in the southern end of the Town waited until she was over 30 years old and became an "old girl" in order to find her ideal man. She finally got her wish and married Mr. Zhang from Chongshi Middle School. Time flies. These young girls are now old, and some may no longer be alive, but their courage to pursue freedom of marriage will always remain in the hearts of the next generation and be widely praised.

小镇一角/A corner in town

十．搬家

说起搬家，这是大家都非常熟悉的一件事，也大都经历过，或从小房子搬到大房子，或从平房搬到楼房，或从乡下搬到城镇，如此等等。一般来说，搬家是件好事情。但对我们父辈来说，搬家却是无奈之举，并且五年搬了五次家，现在想起来令人百感交集，唏嘘不已！

第一次搬家，其实应该说是分家，当然分家的直接后果就是搬家。桑家本是一户大家庭，全家从镇江丹徒搬到双桥镇后，老大一家分开居住另立门户，祖父母带领老二、老三和女儿三家居住在一起，生活在一起。后来，随着孙辈的增多，生意又不景气，日子越过越艰难，分家就成了必然趋势。当地刚解放不久，老三一家首先从大家庭中分离出来，在镇西市稍租了一间门房，开了个小商店，经营烟酒、煤油、糖果等。终因生意萧条，负债累累，落到关门的境地，房租也交不起来，最后只得卷铺盖走人了。

去哪里？搬到何处！首先得解决一家人的栖身之地啊！年迈的奶奶踮着一双小脚来到镇上汪家（土改时评为富农）求援，让我们暂住到他家的田头屋去。所谓田头屋，就是用来存放农具、肥料等，农忙时歇脚吃饭的所在，大都建在大田的边上，平时就空关在那里。于是，第二次搬家就这样开始了。

这两间田头屋在小镇一公里外的乡下，虽是茅草房，比较简陋，但不破不漏，床铺、锅灶、桌凳等还齐全，在这里居住生活还是很不错的。这里的邻居也是挺好的，给我印象最深的是，住在小河北面的郭乡长的母亲特别善良热情。有一次，她家包馄饨，盛了一大碗馄饨，放在木盆里，从小河那边推到这边给我们解馋。

那段时间，在邻居们的帮助下，父亲每天天不亮，鸡叫头遍，就起来和面蒸馒头，然后母亲拿到西界港赶早市去卖。我们就这样度过了那段艰难的岁月。

"东方红，太阳升"。在这里，我们经历了轰轰烈烈的土地改革运动。我们家被评为贫农，分得两间瓦屋和六亩三分土地。从此，我们如梦幻似地突然从"上无片瓦，下无寸土"一跃成了有房有地了！这让我想起俄罗斯大诗人普希金的长篇寓言诗《渔夫和金鱼的故事》，那是寓言，而今天在我们中国竟然成了现实！

这次搬家，也就是第三次搬家，对我们家来说，意义重大，值得大书特书，值得铭记在心！望着两间敞亮的瓦屋，摸着结实的前后门窗，喜悦之情油然而生，心中不禁叫好："我们有家了！""我们终于有了一个属于自己的家了！"

新家在镇南二、三百米的施家宅上，共有二、三十间房屋。现有四户贫农分得了他们多余的房屋，我们家是其中一户。在这里，除了种田，父亲还在夏天到南边贩西瓜，母亲为崇实中学（后改为双桥中学）的老师倒马桶、洗衣服。

父亲做茶食加工是内行，种地就外行了。过往做茶食加工，特别是油煎食品（如煎馓子、炸油绞绞等），长期被油烟所侵，患上了气管炎和哮喘，经常犯病，身子未老先衰。对于务农，既不擅长，更是力不从心，还缺乏生产资料，家里小孩又多，缺乏劳动力。好日子没有持续多久，生活又渐入困境。于是，父亲萌生了重操老本行经商的念头。巧的是，小镇南市稍刘家的三间街面房空关多时，无人问津。机不可失，失不再来，父亲急不可耐地变卖了分得的胜利果实，举家搬到了这里，这该是第四次搬家了！

然而，人算不如天算，当时，镇上有关部门把经商的大门在父亲的面前紧紧关闭了："你们家是农村户口，不能在镇上经商做生意！"一盆冷水把父亲经商的念头彻底浇灭。但一切都晚了，已经没有回头路可走了。

家里是农村户口，但住在镇上，田却在乡下，这种现象在镇上还有不少。于是，有关部门开始清理这种怪象，让他们回归农村，并资助他们在乡下盖房（当然是茅草房）。在走投无路的情况下，父亲不得不接受这种特别的待遇，开始了第五次搬家！

父亲推着载有全部家当的小车往东行驶，一路上大家默默无言，只有车子的呻吟声，似乎在诉说生活的艰难和无奈。小镇渐行渐远，最终在我们的视野和生活中消失。这次搬家终于在这里牢牢地重重地画上了一个圆满的句号！

X. Moving Home

Moving home is familiar to everyone. And almost everyone has experienced it, either from a small house to a bigger one, from a bungalow to a high-rise, or from the countryside to a town or a city, etc. Generally speaking, moving home is a good thing. However, to my father, it had been our only choice. Also, we moved five times in five years, which, coming to think about it, really aroused various feelings in me.

The first move, actually splitting from the big family, happened when we moved from Dantu, Zhenjiang to Shuangqiao Town. The eldest son started his own family. Grandparents lived with the other two sons' and the daughter's families. Later, with more and more grandkids and suffering business, life was harder and harder. Splitting into smaller families became necessary. Soon after the liberation, the third son's family separated from the big family[1]. They rented a street house on the west side of the town and opened a little store to sell cigarettes, wine, kerosene, and candy. The business did not thrive, and the debt grew. So, they had to close the store and leave because they could not even pay the rent.

Where to go? Where to move to? The priority was to find a shelter. Old grandma walked on her bound feet to the Wang's in town—evaluated as a rich peasant in the later Land Reformation—for help. She begged to them so that we could stay in their field shed. The field shed is where people store their tools and fertilizer. Usually built beside the fields, it is also where people take a break and eat during busy farming days. In leisure time, it is not used. Therefore, the second move started this way.

This field shed was in the countryside, one kilometer away from the town. Although it was a simple, straw-thatched shelter, it was not broken or leaking. There were beds, an oven and pots, and a table and benches. It was not bad living there. The neighbors were nice to us as well. What impressed me most was the village director's mom, who lived north of the little

---
1 The third son is "my father."

river. She was very kind and hospitable. Once, her family made dumplings. She put a big bowl of dumplings in a wooden basin and pushed it on the river from her side to our side for us to quell our cravings.

During those days, when the rooster crowed the first time, my father would get up to make steamed buns. Then my mother would take them to the West Border Harbor to sell at the morning fair. Thus, we managed to survive that hard time.

"The east turns red as the sun rises." Here, we experienced the vigorous Land Reformation. My family was evaluated as Poor Peasant; therefore, we were granted a two-room tiled house and 6.3 mu[1] of land. We magically jumped from "not a tile above head or an inch of land below" to owning a house and some land. This reminded me of the great Russian poet Pushkin's long fable poem, "Story of a Fisherman and a Golden Fish." That was a fable, while it became reality today in China.

This move, the third one, was very significant to us. It was worth recording on paper and in the heart. Looking at the two spacious tiled rooms, feeling the sturdy doors and windows, my happiness rose in my heart. "We have a house now! We finally have a house of our own!"

Our new house was on the Shi's estate, which held 20 to 30 houses. Four families, one of which was ours, of Poor Peasants got Shi's extra houses. Here, in addition to farming, my father also sold watermelons in the south in summer. My mother cleaned toilet buckets and did laundry for the teachers at Chongshi Secondary School (later renamed Shuangqiao Secondary School).

Father was good at making snacks, but not so much in farming. In making the snacks, especially those deep-fried ones, such as fried doughs and fried twisters, my father contracted tracheitis and asthma. He constantly had breakouts and got weaker than his age. As stated, he was not good at farming. Additionally, he had a weak physique, lacked means of production and labor, and had a family of seven kids. The good days didn't last long before life went back to hardship. Thus, the idea of resuming <u>the familiar bu</u>siness occurred to him. Coincidentally, the Liu's

---

1 1 mu = 666.7 m², 15 mu = 1 hectare

at the south end of the town had three long-vacant street rooms. Now or never! Father hurriedly sold the assigned house and moved there. This was the fourth move.

However, unlike how he had planned, the town government shut the business door tight in front of Father: "You are of the peasant registration, you can't do business in town!" Like a whole basin of icy water poured down, that put out father's business ambition. Nevertheless, it was too late. There was no way back.

Those who had a rural registration and had plots in the countryside but lived in the town were not uncommon. Therefore, the government started to fix this strange situation to let them return to the countryside. They also helped them build straw-thatched houses in rural areas. With no other options, father had to accept this special treatment and started the fifth move.

Father pushed a wheelbarrow with all the family's possessions to the east. Everybody was quiet, only the moans from the wheelbarrow were "lamenting" all the hardship and unexpectedness of life. The town got farther and farther from us and finally disappeared from our sight, and from our life. This time of moving finally drew a heavy and full stop.

第五次搬到的地方/The fifth move location

十一．起点终点

我们父辈从桑家大家庭（即"共家"）搬出算起，到上世纪50年代初，前前后后有过五次搬家的经历。

一年初春的一天，父亲推着载有全部家当的独轮小车向东迈出第一步的时候，意味着我们第五次搬家开始了。沿着双桥镇北港边的土路，走了一个多小时后，向左拐进了一条小路，来到了一片农田的中心小道，再左拐一百多米，终于停在了两间新盖的茅草房门前。这个茅草房是人民公社免费为动迁户建造的。那时候，安排全家是农业户口但居住在城镇的居民迁移到东部长江边围垦区的，称之为"东迁"。我们家就是其中的一户。这就是我们从此要居住、生活的地方。

小车刚一停下来，邻居们纷纷走出各自的家门围了过来，他们可能怀着不同的心绪，默默地看着这一家子，似乎在欣赏外星人。开始是窃窃私语，后来声音也就越来越大。一位大嫂（后来知道她姓陆）首先发难，大声嚷道："在镇上不好好做生意，到我们乡下做啥？"帮腔的说"就是呀，还小倌[1]多，只晓得吃，又不会干活，到我们这里抢饭吃啊！"你一句我一句的，有嘲讽的，也有骂的，大有不让我们在这里安家、立即赶走我们的架势。这时，一位婶娘（后来知道这是隔壁的陈家阿婆）说话了："都讲啥呀，人家在镇上好好的是不会来我们乡下的。人家也不容易，还带了几个小倌，作孽啊。"最后是一位大伯（后来知道是金队长）吼道："人家招你们惹你们啦，在这里瞎三话四！走，走，快走开！" 这种罕见的"欢迎"，给我们留下了深刻的不可名状的印象。

草屋不大，也不算小。四壁都是芦苇墙，中间也是篱笆隔开，分为房间和灶间两间。房间向东的一面开了一个小窗户，但没有玻璃，用一把破旧的芭蕉扇插在上面当窗棂，整个房间黑乎乎的，外面一间就是灶间。开始的时候，这里也没有砌灶头，就用原来烤贴大饼的炉子倒置过来，经过简易加工，就成了一个"行灶"。一个行灶，烧饭炒菜都用它。烧火的时候，整个灶间烟雾腾腾，呛得人咳嗽流眼泪。特别是烧火的人首当其冲，眼泪鼻涕一大把，好不狼狈。我们在这里的生活就是在烟雾中拉开了序幕的。

俗话说，路遥知马力，日久见人心。在人生地不熟的环境里，

---

[1] 小倌：当地方言，意为小孩。

我们初来乍到，要认识和了解邻居们。同样，邻居们也要认识和了解我们。时间是最好的磨合剂和见证者。

有一次，陆大嫂的孩子突发高烧，家里又没有其他人，她急得像热锅上的蚂蚁，手足无措。小孩哭，她也哭。他们的哭声被父亲听到了，父亲立即赶过去。问明情况后，二话不说，当即抱着她孩子，同她一路步行，赶到离家三公里左右的东界港卫生室。医生立马给孩子吊针，经及时医治，孩子转危为安。孩子母亲流泪了，不知是高兴，还是感动，或许兼而有之。她从此总是念叨桑家伯伯的好。

为了翻修茅草房，父亲和队长骑着自行车，合伙到三十多公里外的塘桥、杨舍一带去购买建筑材料，拉回来一批橡子。怎么分呢？父亲诚恳地对队长说："你先拣，剩下的归我。"这件事，曾一度在全村传为佳话。

在吃大食堂的日子里，村民们对饭菜特别是早餐的粥意见很大。"水是水，米是米，这是什么粥啊？"后来父亲去掌勺，同样多的米，烧出来的粥又稠又糯，既好吃又耐饥。大家吃得高兴，最后把碗底都舔得干干净净。

当时，在当地，父亲算是有点文化的；又似乎见多识广，还能说会道，于是成了全村的一个权威了。大家有什么事情，譬如说婚丧嫁娶之类，都来找桑家伯伯商议、拍板。后来，连夫妻不和、兄弟姐妹争端、父子反目等等，也找父亲当"老娘舅"来调解。结果大多拉手言和，笑脸相对，满意而归。村上被正式任命的调解员反而无所事事，形同虚设，有时候还暗生妒意。

母亲也用自己的为人和言行赢得了大家的认可和称赞。干活时，她脏活累活抢着干，不挑不拣。在水利工地上，她同男劳力一样挖泥、挑泥，被工地评为劳动模范。后来，她同陈家阿婆一起帮生产队里幼儿园带孩子，以致多年后孩子们长大了还口口声声唤她"桑家奶奶"。

我们做子女的都算争气，也都努力。首先是老二，响应政府支边号召，16、7岁就从这里背井离乡，只身去数千公里之外的新疆石河子工作。老大从这里考上了北京的一所知名大学。老六更是发奋图强，高中没上一天竟然也从这里考取了南京的一所高校。其他姐妹也都通过各自的努力开辟了自己的天地。如果说，我们父辈第五次也是最后一次搬家到这里，算是终点；那我们做子女的则把这里变成了起点，从这里走向了更为广阔的人生旅程。

XI. Ending Point, Starting Point

My father relocated five times, since the separation from the big family to the beginning of 1950s.

One day in early spring, my father stepped to the east with his single-wheeled cart filled with our belongings, which signified our fifth move. After walking along the dirt road on the north side of Shuangqiao Town for about an hour, turning left to a little road which became a center road in the farming fields, turning left again and walking for about 100 meters, he finally stopped in front of a two-room newly-built thatched hut. It was built by the People's Commune for the migrants for free. At that time, they were used to arrange those so-called "East-Movers," who were the rural households but lived in the town and later moved to the reclamation area in the east, close to the Yangtze River. My family was one of them. This would be the place we would be living and residing from then on.

The moment the cart stopped, the neighbors came out of their houses and came close, staring at us. Probably with different thoughts, they first watched us silently as if looking at some E.T.s. Then they started to exchange some talk, first quietly, then louder and louder. A woman (later known as surnamed Lu) started to attack us by shouting, "Why are you here instead of doing your business in town?" Some chimed in, "Exactly. With so many kids who eat but not work, are you trying to steal our food?!" More comments came along, sarcasm, cussing. It seemed that they wanted to drive us away and not let us settle here. At that time, another aunt (later we learned she was the neighbor Chen's Granny) said, "What are you all talking about? They wouldn't come here if they were doing good in town. It was not easy for them, not to mention the little kids. What a shame." Finally, an uncle (later we learned he was the village leader) yelled at them, "They didn't do anything wrong to you that deserves your nonsensical comments! Go away, go, go, hurry!" This unusual "welcome" left a deep and indescribable impression on us.

The hut was neither big nor small. The walls were made of

reed which also separated the bedroom from the kitchen and living room. There opened a little window on the east side of the bedroom, but without glass. A broken banana leaf fan stood there as the window lattice. The whole room looked dark. The outside room was the kitchen and living room. In the beginning, there was no stove built. It was a remodeled upside-down stove used for making cookies, called a "portable stove." Such a stove was used by us to make both rice and other dishes. When cooking, the whole room was smokey, which made people cough and shed tears, especially those who sat there keeping the fire. They usually got very embarrassed by their tears and snot. Just in this cooking smoke, our life here started.

There's a saying that distance knows horses' strength and time tells people's heart. In the strange and new environment, we were the newcomers and needed to know our neighbors. Vice versa, our neighbors needed to know us. Time is the best grinding agent and witness.

One day, Mrs. Lu's kid got a high fever. Without other family members around, she was as anxious as an ant on a hot pan. Not knowing what to do, she cried together with her kid. Their chaos was heard by my father who went over immediately. After knowing what was going on, he held the child to walk with her to the clinic in the East Border Harbor three kilometers away from home. The doctor gave the kid an IV right away. The swift treatment saved the child. Mrs. Lu shed tears again. We did not know it was due to being happy or moved, maybe both. After that incident, she always talked about how good the uncle at Sang's was.

In order to renovate the hut, father and the village leader went to Tangqiao and Yangshe on bikes together to buy construction materials. They bought some rafters. But how were they gonna divide between them? Father said to the leader sincerely, "You pick first, the rest is mine." This incident was once spread as a nice story in the whole village.

In the days of eating in the village communal canteen, the residents were very unsatisfied with the meals, especially the porridge for breakfast. "Water and rice are separate. What kind of porridge is that?" Later, my father went to cook there. With the same amount of rice, his porridge was thick and chewy, delicious and hunger-reducing. Everybody was happy and even licked the bottom of the bowl.

At that time, my father was somewhat educated, and he seemed to know a lot and was articulate. Thus, he became an authority for the whole village. If the villagers had some issues, such as a wedding, funeral, etc., they all came to consult with "Sang's Uncle." Later, even for domestic squabbles, sibling disputes, and father-son arguments, etc., they all came to father for mitigation. Those mostly resulted in hand-shaking, smiling, and satisfaction. The appointed mitigator for the village, instead, had nothing to do. With the empty title, sometimes he would be jealous.

My mother also won people's acknowledgement and praise with her actions and words. In farm work, she would take the initiative to do dirty and heavy work, never picky. On water conservancy work, she dug and carried mud like a man, which earned her a "model worker" title on the site. Later, she worked in the village kindergarten together with Chen's Granny, so much so that the children she helped always addressed her as "Sang's Grandma," even after they grew up.

Kids like us were also working hard. The second kid, who left home alone at around 16 to 17, responding to the government's call for supporting the borders, went to work at Shihezi, Xinjiang, thousands of miles away northwest. The first kid got admitted into a well-known college in Beijing. The sixth kid was even more hard-working. He got admitted into a college in Nanjing without even having one day of high school education. The other sisters also started their own life through their efforts. If we say that father's fifth and also last relocation to here was the final destination, then we kids transformed it into a starting point, where we walked to an even broader life journey.

十二．家乡的小河

家乡的小河和家乡的小路一样纵横交错，四通八达。特别是家乡的小河，同当地的人们关系密切，息息相关。几十年过去了，家乡的小河时不时地在我心中流淌，在我梦中流淌，因为那里有我童年的身影和欢乐。

如果说草原上的人们是逐草而居，那我们家乡的人们则是逐水而居。不是房前就是屋后，就会有小河流淌。就拿我的出生地双桥镇来说，也有两条河，见证着小镇过往的繁荣和衰败。镇北有一条东西向的小河，镇中有一条南北向的小河，把小镇分成东西两大部分，镇北那条小河由东直通长江。她就在我家边上流过，潮涨潮落几十年，南北方向的小河可直达乐余、鹿苑、常熟等。两条小河交汇在镇中的桥下，形成丁字形。

南来的货船，装有缸、盆、瓷器之类，常停靠在镇中桥堍头，供人们挑选。最抢手的就是缸了，其用途非常广泛，可用作水缸、米缸、酒缸等等。特别是水缸，不管是镇上或是乡下，几乎家家都有一口放在灶头边，里面装满从河里挑上来的水。把明矾碾成粉末，视水缸大小，放入适量的明矾粉末，用擀面杖搅匀。不一会儿，水缸里的水清澈如镜，就可用来烧水做饭了。当时特别是乡下，常有路人向路边人家讨水喝，"问你们要点水喝喝。" 主人也慷慨应允。于是路人拿起灶头上的水瓢，揭开水缸盖，舀起缸里的水就往嘴里灌。喝完一抹嘴，满意地边道谢边继续赶路了。看路人喝水的劲头，胜过当今喝纯净水、可口可乐。

平时人们生活用水离不开河水，种田如育秧、插秧、种水稻更是离不开河水了。当时，人们在河边架起水车，长长的水闸从河边伸入河中。中间如链条似的，用一片片小木板把水刮上来，灌进稻田。水车用四组脚蹬相接，上面站着四人，同时力踩蹬，把水车上来。有时我们小孩子也参与其中，因体力、腿短等等原因，跟不上大人、大小孩踩蹬的节奏和速度，时有"吊田鸡"的事情发生。就是双手紧挂在横杆上，双脚踩空，悬在空中，此谓"吊田鸡"也。我也被"吊"过几次，又怕又高兴，想哭更想笑。

冬季来临之际，家乡的农民非常勤快，开始放水挖河泥了。这时雨水少，河水也少，又是冬闲，乡亲们在河边架起水车，把水车到另一条小河里。这里的水车干了，就开始挖泥挑泥，堆在河边，待开春再往大田里均匀散开，这是上等肥料，比后来的化肥等不知强多少倍。在一次挖泥时，我亲眼看见有趣的一幕，隔壁黄某挖着挖着，突然弯腰把混在泥水中的一包什么东西捡起来，一声不吭地飞快跑回家中。这是一包什么东西呢？他一直到死也没有公开说过。这个谜随他一起埋进了历史的烟雨中。

　　土改结束后的第一个冬天，天气特别暖和。这时的村民组长提议把地主最后那部分浮财分掉，这浮财就是水产：围养在宅基四周小河里的鱼类。说干就干，这里也用上了水车，村民们一家出一人，打坝的打坝，车水的车水。随着河水越来越少，河里的大鱼小鱼跃跃欲跳出水面，活蹦乱跳。村民们用大小不一的木盆在水中抓鱼。岸边观看的大人小孩欢呼雀跃，一片欢腾笑语，比过年还热闹。最后村民们把鱼都集中在晒场上，村民组长指挥大家分鱼。这是胜利果实啊，根据村民小组的户数分成若干堆大小，均匀分配，然后抽签对号领取自己应得的一份鱼。大多数是鲢鱼，我们乡下人称为白鱼。小的一斤左右，大的有两三斤。每家分得十多斤，还不算小鱼小虾之类，家家户户喜气洋洋，大人小孩都沉浸在喜悦之中。

　　在美好的氛围中，可惜还存在不和谐的事情。那就是大家在忙着抓鱼的过程中，住在河西的李某（当时大家都把他看成"刺儿头"、"二流子"）偷偷地抱起一条最大的白鱼就往家跑。组长和村民们都看在眼里，敢怒不敢言，怕不要因为一条鱼而破坏了当时美好的气氛。更怕今后他惹是生非，弄得整个村民小组不得安宁。大家的宽容使他脸面无存，无地自容。

　　家乡的小河也是我们小孩子们的活动舞台（主要在夏天）。一天，我们在做完早操准备上课的时候，一位老师把一个小学生推上讲台，这个宋姓学生低着头，身后插着一根芦苇，上面还吊着一只挣扎着的大虾。老师批评他晨读时不看书，却跑到河边钓虾。本是告诫大家，实际却把他当成了我们的榜样啊，原来可以用芦苇捉虾的。我后来也试了几次，也还算成功。在我们家经济困难的岁月里，我在河里摸过蟹、钓过鳗鲡，每次还都有所收获，解了全家的馋。一天，我们几个小孩子在双桥镇镇北的那条河里摸黄蚬（贝壳类的东西），突然大家都停下来往桥上看去，原来镇西开豆腐店的丫头手里拿着簸箕，正站在桥中央向桥下倒什么东西。一个黑乎乎的东西顷刻掉进了河里，还发出了吱吱的叫声。后来知道那丫头原以为小猪死了，把它倒进河里，而小猪没有死，倒进河里才真正淹死了。

家乡的小河默默地，无私地给人们带来了诸多益处，说不尽道不完，所以给我留下了永远的思念。但待我退休回家，已不见了当时小河的风采。既没有了鱼虾，也没有了水流的琴弦般的声响，有的则是浑浊不堪的污水在随风飘荡，似在哭诉，似在呜咽。双桥镇中两河交汇处的那座桥梁被拆掉，被泥石的路坝所代替，南北向的小河被截断：既断了它的来路，又断了它的出路。我还听说邻居家的黄花闺女学父亲驾船电鱼，不幸触电身亡。这些悲剧是怎么造成的？谁造成的？真不知道应该追究谁的责任了。

俗话说得好："一方水土养一方人"。人类是靠水土养育的，方能生存、繁衍下去。并且水土、水土，水在前，可见水之重要！我们应该对包括小河在内的大自然有敬畏之心，更应该有感恩之心，进而好好善待它们，保护它们，这是惠及人们当下乃至子孙后代的大好事。

镇上小河/River at Shuangqiao

XII. The Rivers in my Hometown

The small rivers in my hometown are as crisscrossed and well-connected as the small roads there. They are closely related to the local people. Decades have passed, and the small rivers in my hometown flow in my heart and in my dreams from time to time, as they reflect my childhood experiences and joys.

If people on the grassland look for grass to live by, then people in our hometown are after water. There is always a stream flowing either in front of or behind their houses. Take Shuangqiao Town, where I was born, for example: There are two rivers. They have witnessed the prosperity and decline of the town. Besides a small river running east-west in the north of the town, there's also a small river running north-south in the center of the town, dividing the town into two major parts, east and west. The small river in the north of the town goes directly to the Yangtze River to the east. She flows right by my house, with the tides rising and falling for decades. The small river running north and south can directly reach Leyu, Luyuan, Changshu, etc. The two small rivers meet under the bridge in the town, forming a T shape.

Cargo ships coming from the south, loaded with jars, basins, porcelain, etc., often docked at the end of the bridge in the town to sell their goods. The most popular was the jar, which had a wide range of uses such as holding water, rice, wine, etc. Especially the water jar, whether in the town or in the countryside, almost every family had one next to the stove, filled with water carried from the river. People ground alum into powder, added the appropriate amount of the powder depending on the size of the water tank, and stirred it with a rolling pin. After a while, the water in the water tank was as clear as a mirror and could be used to drink or cook. At that time, especially in the countryside, passers-by often asked for water from the households on the roadside, "I would like some water from you." The owner also generously agreed. So, the passer-by picked up the ladle on the stove, opened the lid of the water tank, scooped up some water from the tank, and poured it into his mouth. After drinking, he wiped his mouth, thanked the owner with satisfaction and continued his journey. The enjoyment of the passers-by drinking water trump those drinking purified water or Coca-Cola today.

People there could not live without river water, and farming—such as raising seedlings, transplanting rice, and planting rice—could not live without river water even more so. At that time, people set up water wheels by the river, and long sluice gates extended from the riverside into the river. In the middle, like a chain, small wooden boards were used to scrape water up and pour it into the rice paddies. The water wheel was connected by four sets of pedals, and four people stood on it, stepping on the pedals synchronically to bring the water up. Sometimes we children also participated. Due to physical strength and our short height, among other things, we could not keep up with the rhythm and speed of adults and older kids stepping on the pedals. Sometimes "Hanging Frogs" happened, that is, both of our hands were tightly hung on the horizontal bar, with both feet hanging in the air, looking like a frog hung on the bar, therefore the name. I have also been "hung" several times, afraid but excited, and I wanted to cry but more to laugh.

When winter came, the farmers in my hometown were very diligent and began to release water and dig river mud. During this time, there was little rain or river water, and there was not much farming work, so the villagers set up a waterwheel by the river and moved the water into another small river. When this river was dry, they began to dig mud and pile it by the river, and then spread it evenly in the fields in spring. This is a high-quality fertilizer, which is many times better than modern chemical fertilizers. During one mud digging, I saw an interesting scene with my own eyes. Huang living next door, while digging, suddenly bent down to pick up a bag of something mixed in the mud and water, and ran back home quickly without saying a word. What was in this bag? He never said it publicly in his life. This mystery was buried with him in the mist and rain of history.

The first winter after the Land Reform was particularly warm. The village leader proposed to divide up the last part of the landlords' floating wealth, which was aquatic products—fish raised in the small river around the homestead. They did it right away. Waterwheels were also used. One person from each family worked to build dams and to pull water out. As the water in the river diminished, fish of various sizes in the river jumped around. The villagers used all kinds of wooden basins to catch the fish in the river. The adults and children watching on the shore cheered and laughed, which was more lively than the New Year. Finally, the villagers gathered all the fish in the drying yard, and the village leader directed everyone to deal with the fruits of victory. They were divided into several piles of different sizes according to the number of households in the village, evenly distributed, and then they drew lots to pick up their share. Most of the fish were silver carps, which we call white fish. The small ones weighed about one pound, and the big ones two or three pounds. Each family got more than 10 pounds, in addition to the small fish and shrimps. Every household was in high spirits, and adults and children immersed in joy.

In the exuberant atmosphere, unfortunately, there was still something disharmonious. That was, when everyone was busy catching fish, Li, who lived to the west of the river, regarded as a "thorn" and a "second-rate person" by everyone at the time, secretly picked up the biggest white fish and ran home. The team leader and the villagers saw it, but dared not speak out, fearing that a fish would destroy the nice atmosphere. They were even more afraid he would cause more trouble in the future and make the whole village group restless. Everyone's tolerance made him lose face and feel ashamed.

The small rivers in my hometown were also playgrounds for us kids (mainly in summer). One day, when we had finished our morning exercises and were preparing for class, a teacher pushed a primary school student onto the front. This student, surnamed Song, lowered his head, with a reed stuck behind him, and a struggling prawn hanging on it. The teacher criticized him for not reading during morning reading time but going to the river to fish for prawns. It was meant to be a warning to everyone, but he actually became our role model. It turned out that you could catch prawns with reeds. I tried it a few times later, and was quite successful. During the years when our family was in financial difficulties, I caught crabs and eels in the river, and each time I would catch something, which satisfied the cravings of the whole family. One day, several of us kids were catching yellow clams in the river at the north of Shuangqiao Town. Suddenly everyone stopped and looked up at the bridge. We saw the girl from the tofu shop in the west of the town was holding a dustpan in her hand, standing in the middle of the bridge and pouring something down. A black thing fell into the river in an instant, and it made a squeaking sound. Later we learned that the girl thought the piglet was dead and dumped it into the river, but the piglet was not dead and was drowned after it was dumped into the water.

The small rivers in my hometown have silently and selflessly brought many benefits to people, which are too numerous to exhaust, so it's left me with eternal longing. But after I was retired and went home, the charm of the small rivers at that time was gone. There were no fish or shrimps, and no sound of the water like strings. Instead, there was muddy sewage floating in the wind, as if crying and sobbing. The bridge at the intersection of the two rivers in Shuangqiao Town was demolished and replaced by a mud and stone road dam, and the small river running north and south was cut off; it cut off both its way in and its way out. I also heard that the young girl of a neighbor's family had learned from her father to drive a boat to electrocute fish, but unfortunately died of electrocution. How did all these tragedies happen? Who is to blame? I really don't know.

As the saying goes, "the local water and land nurture the local people." Human beings rely on them to survive and reproduce.

And when we say "water and land," water comes first, which shows how important water is. We should have awe for nature, including the river, and we should be grateful, and treat it well and protect it. It benefits people of current and future generations.

长江一角/The Yangtze River

十三．童年纪事

每个人都有童年，并且都给自己留下了美好的难忘的记忆：或酸，或甜，或苦，或辣，五味杂陈，终生不忘。但我的童年与众不太一样，可谓之冰火两重天。

我出身在一个经商的家庭里，我的祖母生养了三个儿子和一个女儿，并且都已结婚生子。大儿子结婚早，一连生育了三位"千金"，老二家的头胎也是女孩儿。幸亏有女儿，一连生育了两个儿子，给当时男尊女卑思想较为严重的祖母来说，或许平添了不少的安慰，但一个"外"字总是在心里留下了抹不去的阴影。

幸运之神终于降临到桑家的头上，老三媳妇一连生育了两个儿子，只用了两年时间。祖母整天乐得合不拢嘴，她踮着莲步，给左邻右舍、诸亲好友发送了红蛋，似乎向世界昭示：桑家有后了，桑家后继有人了！

遗憾的是，大孙子因先天不足，疾病缠身，四、五岁时就夭折了。幸亏上天留下了我，身价顿时提高了，由二孙子上升到大孙子，全家把所有的爱都聚集到我一个人身上。特别是祖母，她一有空，就来抱我，嘴里用浓重的镇江话不停地念叨着："我的老小，我的老小……"，让我吃好的，穿好的，不让我挨冻受饿，不让我受一点点委屈。

就这样，我在蜜罐里生，在蜜罐里长，开始了自己的童年生活。也正因为如此，我也养成了很多不好的习惯，特别是在吃的方面，非常挑食：不吃蔬菜，不吃面条，不吃菜饭，每遇到家里吃面条或菜饭，祖母总是想办法帮我"解危"，大多是叫隔壁的老大媳妇（我叫他大妈妈）把他们家做的饭菜端过来给我吃。

在吃零食方面更是"讲究"，一般的馓子、油绞绞、脆饼等尝都不尝。吃月饼，只吃细沙（豆沙）月饼，其他的不屑一顾。

然而，好景不长！我们老三一家终于从大家庭中分出来了。我们搬到了双桥镇西市梢一个出租屋里，开起了小商店。当时经商很不景气，我们的小店慢慢衰败破产，最终达到了关门歇业的地步，一家人的生计就成了大问题。

我记得很清楚：一个冬天的早晨，母亲抱着小菊坐在桌子边的一条长凳子上，目光呆滞，默默地盯着冷灶冷锅。我和淑莲也木木地坐在一边，一声不吭，只是用饥渴的眼神望着母亲。我们心里都清楚：这天的早饭没有做，也没有米可做。父亲不知道什么时候出去了，也许又到诸亲好友家"东捞西借"去了吧。这时，邻居李家的大儿子来我家玩，看到了我们一家的境况，似乎明白了什么，立即回家。不一会儿，他拿来了一碗大米，把碗放到了桌上。母亲无奈地笑着，回绝了邻居家的好意，硬是叫他把米端了回去。我们非常不解地望着母亲，大家就这样度过了这个寒冷又饥饿的早晨。

由于多时未交房租，房东忍无可忍地下达了"逐客令"，限我们先是一周内后又延迟了三天需要搬走。另租房，没有钱，也一时找不到合适的房源。怎么办？"总不能让我们一家接络子上天吧！"母亲几近绝望地哀叹着。祖母得知我们的近况后，厚着脸皮，踮着莲步，到镇上富农汪家求情，让我们暂住到他们家的田头屋里。

为了解决生计问题，在好心人的指点和帮助下，父亲借来了笼屉，重操旧业，决定蒸馒头卖。从此，每天天不亮，父母亲就早早起床忙开了。父亲揉面做馒头，母亲坐在灶膛烧火。馒头蒸好后，母亲把我从睡梦中叫醒，父亲把馒头一一装在大淘箩里，上面用毛巾和小棉袄盖好。接着母亲就拎着装满馒头的淘箩，带着我，走进了濛濛的晨雾中，去西界港赶早市。西界港离家有二、三里路，我们高一脚低一脚地走着，路上几乎见不到一个行人。在集上，我们来回走着，一边叫卖。刚开始的时候，馒头好卖，用不了多久就会卖光。后来，也有人做这生意了，有了竞争者，馒头就不好卖了。他们还低价出售，本来一分钱一个馒头，他们还五分钱卖六个，以此吸引人。我们无奈也只得这样做，不仅赚钱少了，还有时卖不出去。

真是祸不单行。正当我们为卖馒头犯难的时候，一天父亲把馒头蒸砸了：许是碱水放多了，馒头发黄，大多没有发出来，成了死面疙瘩。这当然不能卖了，只得我们自己吃，一天三顿饭就吃这样的馒头，个中滋味只有当事人心知肚明。

远逝的童年经历了很多很多，但总有几件事让人一生都忘不掉，至今我还记忆犹新，历历在目，永远定格在脑海深处。

那天早晨的断顿没饭吃和后来啃着死面疙瘩当饭吃，同早些时候我这个不吃那个不吃，形成了多么多么鲜明的对照啊！这简直是对我的极大嘲弄和绝妙的讽刺。这是生活同我开了一个不大不小的玩笑，其实是生活给我上了一堂生动而深刻的不可或缺的重要一课。我应该敬畏生活，更应该感谢生活！

XIII. Childhood Chronicles

Everyone has his or her own childhood that leaves them beautiful and unforgettable memories: sour, sweet, bitter, spicy, mixed with all kinds of flavors, remembered for a lifetime. But my childhood is different from others; it can be described as ice and fire.

I was born in a business family. My grandmother gave birth to three sons and one daughter, and they were all married and had children. The eldest son got married early and gave birth to three daughters in a row. The first child of the second son's family was also a girl. Fortunately, the daughter gave birth to two sons, which might have provided some comfort to my grandmother, who had a very stubborn idea of male superiority and female inferiority at that time, but the fact that the grandsons wouldn't be able to carry the surname always left an indelible shadow in her heart.

Luck finally descended on the Sang family. The third daughter-in-law gave birth to two sons consecutively in just two years. Grandma was so happy that all day she couldn't stop smiling. She walked with her bound feet, or "lotus" steps, and gave red eggs[1] to neighbors, relatives and friends, as if to show the world: the Sang family finally had successors.

Unfortunately, the eldest grandson died at the age of four or five due to congenital deficiencies and illnesses. Fortunately, God left me, the second grandson, to survive, and my status in the family increased tremendously. I rose from the second grandson to the eldest grandson, and the whole family put all their love on me. Especially my grandmother, who would come to hold me whenever she was free and kept chanting in a thick Zhenjiang dialect accent: "My beloved, my beloved...," letting me eat well and wear good clothes, and not allowing me to bear any discomfort of cold or hunger, or any little grievance.

Just like that, I was born and raised in a "honey pot," which featured my childhood. And just because of this, I also

---

[1] Giving red-dyed hard-boiled eggs to relatives and friends is the custom for families who has just got a new baby. Red is a color of good luck, happiness, and prosperity, while the egg itself symbolizes fertility, birth, and new beginnings.

developed many bad habits, especially in terms of eating. I was very picky about food: I wouldn't eat vegetables, noodles, or veggie rice. Whenever we ate noodles or veggie rice, my grandmother would always find a way to help me "get out of trouble," mostly by asking her eldest daughter-in-law next door (I address her as Big Mama) to bring me some of the food they cooked.

I was even more "peculiar" about snacks. I would not even try the usual Sanzi, Yougaogao (now called Mahua), crispy biscuits, etc. When eating mooncakes, I only ate mooncakes with fine red bean paste and disdained the other types.

However, good times never last. Our small family later separated from the big family. We moved to a rented house in the west end of Shuangqiao Town and opened a small shop. At that time, business was very difficult, and our small shop gradually declined and went bankrupt, until reaching the point of closing down. The survival of the family became a big problem.

I remember it very clearly: One winter morning, my mother, eyes dull, silently stared at the cold stove and cold pot, sitting on a bench by the table holding my sister Xiaoju. My other sister Shulian and I also sat numbly on the side, without saying a word, just looking at our mother with hungry eyes. We all knew in our hearts that breakfast was not cooked that day, and that there was no rice to cook with. I don't know when my father went out, maybe to our relatives' and friends' homes to "borrow." Then, the eldest son of the neighbor Li's dropped by. He looked at us, seemed to understand something, and immediately went out. After a while, he brought a bowl of rice grain and put it on the table. Mother smiled helplessly and rejected the neighbor's kindness, insisting that he take the rice back. We looked at her in confusion and thus spent that morning cold and hungry.

As we had not paid the rent for a long time, the landlord could no longer bear it and issued an eviction order, demanding we move out within a week, later extended the deadline for another three days. We had no money to rent another house, and we could not find a suitable place for the time being. What should we do? "We can't let our family go to hell." Mother lamented in despair. After learning about our situation, my grandmother thickened her face, went to the rich farmer Wang's family in town to plead for us to stay in their farmhouse temporarily.

In order to survive, with the guidance and help of some kind people, my father borrowed a steamer and resumed his old business—steaming buns to sell. From then on, my parents got up early every day before dawn. My father kneaded the dough to make buns, and my mother sat behind the stove to keep the fire. After the buns were cooked, Mother woke me up from my sleep, and Father put the buns one by one in a large basket, covering them with a towel and a cotton-stuffed jacket. Then my mother carried the basket and took me into the misty fog to go to the morning market at West Border Harbor, about one mile away from home. We stumbled on the road where there was hardly a single pedestrian. At the market, we walked back and forth, shouting about our buns. At the beginning, steamed buns were easy to sell and would be sold out in a short time. Later, some others started this business also. And with competitors, steamed buns became difficult to sell. They also decreased the price. Originally, one steamed bun cost one cent, but they would sell six for five cents to attract customers. We had no choice but to do likewise. Not only did we make less money, but sometimes we couldn't even sell them.

Misfortunes never come alone. Just when we were having trouble selling steamed buns, one day my father made a mess of the steamed buns: perhaps too much lye was added, the buns turned yellow, and most of them didn't rise, becoming dead dough lumps. Of course, we couldn't sell them, so we had to eat them ourselves. We ate such buns for three meals a day. Only those who have lived this can understand the taste and the feeling.

There are many things in childhood that have passed by, but there are always a few things that people will never forget. I still remember those moments vividly, and they are forever fixed in the depths of my mind.

The lack of food that morning and the eating of dead dough as food later formed such a sharp contrast with my being a picky eater earlier. This was simply a great mockery and a wonderful irony to me. It was a big joke played by life on me, but in fact, life taught me a vivid, profound, and indispensable important lesson. I should respect life, and even more so, I should be grateful for life.

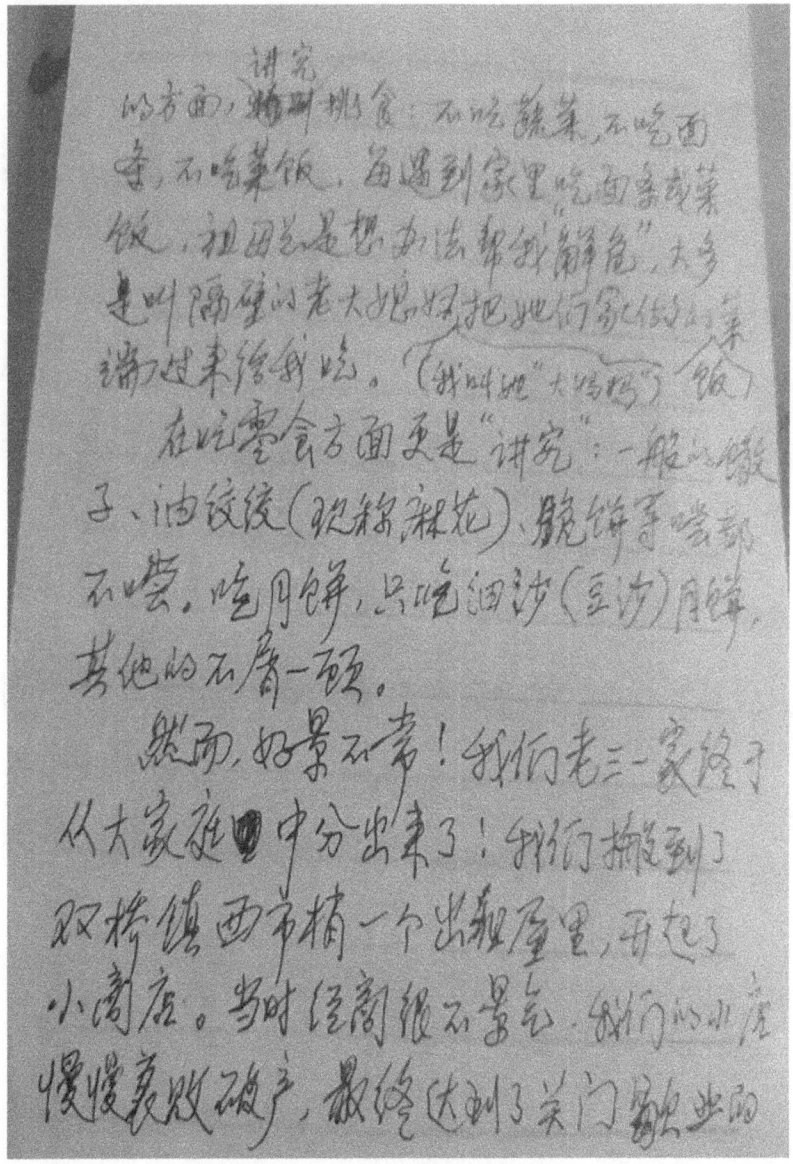

第二部分 叙事诗
Narrative Poetry

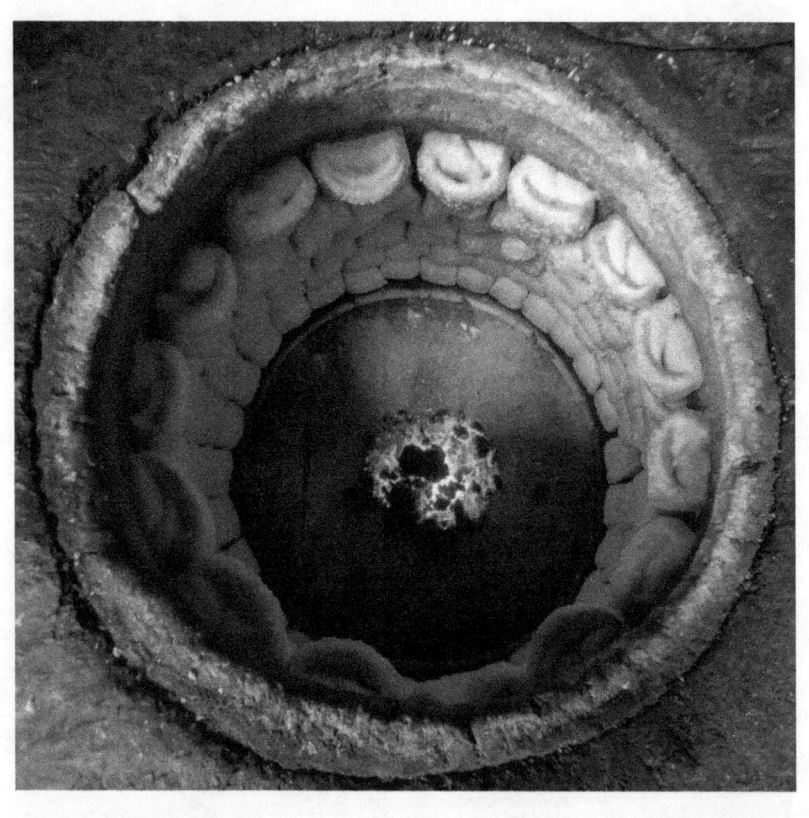

第一章
小镇安家

装载着一家老少和全部家当,
装载着对明天的憧憬和向往,
从镇江丹徒雇船起航,
桑家沿江而下,驶向东方。

告别祖辈传下来的一屋一房,
告别左邻右舍的大伯大娘,
老板频频回首一脸忧伤,
老板娘桑周氏一双泪眼凝望家乡。

丹徒小镇座落在长江边上,
桑家世世代代在这里经商,
做人要仗义,生意才兴隆,
义隆招牌高挂在店堂。

桑家茶食的名声很响,
顾客总是盈门满堂,
生意越做越红火,
财源滚滚在这里流淌。

俗话说:人怕出名猪怕壮,
飞来的暗箭来自同行,
地痞流氓也常来捣乱,
闹得生意难做人心惶惶。

"糕点霉变",诬陷栽赃,
"偷漏税款,扰乱市场",
莫须有的罪名
像脏水泼在身上,像绳索套在脖子上。

老板愁容满面担心生意泡汤,
桑周氏唉声叹气心里发慌,
孩子们没有了欢声笑语,

一家人陷入了困境和绝望。

惹不起还能躲不起,
三十六计还是走为上,
当家人最后咬牙拍板,
举家东迁出外闯一闯。

桑周氏弟弟多年在上海闯荡,
曾多次召唤他们去那边经商;
他们从他的身上
看到了一家未来的希望。

上海成了他们前去的方向,
帆船在江面上乘风破浪,
一家人在心中默默祈祷,
在上海重振家业创造辉煌。

然而,天有不测风云,
途中狂风暴雨突然来临,
船在江面上东摇西晃,
人在舱里东倒西歪呕吐不尽。

船老大处惊不乱降帆把舵,
迅速把船驶近江边靠岸藏躲,
后来驶进了一条小河大桥下面,
在这里遮风挡雨避免灾祸。

Chapter One
Settling Down in Shuangqiao

Carrying a family of young, old, and all belongings,
Loaded with tomorrow's longings,
The boat hired from Dantu, Zhenjiang,
Down the river towards the east, the Sangs were sailing.

Farewell to the houses passed down from ancestors,
Farewell to the uncles and aunts and the neighbors,
The husband frequently turned around sadly,
The wife looked at her hometown tearfully.

The small town of Dantu sits on the edge of the Yangtze River.
The Sangs had been doing business for generations here.
The Yilong signboard hung high in the store.
Only by being righteous can your business prosper.

Sang's tea snacks had a very good reputation.
The house was always full of customers,
The business got more and more booming,
Money and wealth were rolling and flowing.

As the saying goes:
Men are afraid of being famous, like pigs being fat.
The arrows flew from fellow jealous businessmen,
Ruffians also came to look for trouble.

"Moldy pastry," "Tax evasion," "Market disrupting,"
Unfounded charges were like dirty water splashed,
Like a rope around the neck.
Business was hard to carry on.

The boss was worried about the trade.
Mrs. Zhou-Sang sighed and panicked.
The children no longer had joy,

The whole family was in trouble and despair.

If you can't attack, you can at least hide.
Evading is always a better strategy.
The family finally clenched their teeth and made the decision:
Moving eastward to try their fortune.

Zhou-Sang's younger brother had been living in Shanghai
for long, who had summoned them many times
to do business there; From him,
They saw hope for the family's future.

With Shanghai the destination,
The sailboat rode on the wind and waves,
The family in their hearts silently prayed,
To revitalize the family craft in Shanghai.

However, something unexpected happened.
A violent storm suddenly occurred.
The boat swayed on the river.
Passengers staggered around and puked.

Not panicking,
The ship owner lowered the sails and steered the helm.
Quickly drove the boat to the shore,
Later he sailed it under a bridge for shelter.

第二章
苦心经营

河岸上竟是建设中的双桥小镇,
东西一条主街有两里路长,
有米行、布店、肉铺和药房,
短缺的是茶食糕点的作坊。

是留在这里还是继续东去,
一时大家都心中无数,
女婿李生看了街面连连摇头,
"这小地方太受委屈!"

老板身体不佳愁眉不展,
桑周氏踮着莲步桌前一站:
"天菩萨把我们送到这里,
顺从天意,我们就在这里开店设摊!"

桑义隆的金字招牌,
竖在小镇十字街头多年不败,
从此这里的茶食糕点,
翻开了新的一页,开启了新的一代。

烤有脆饼、蛋糕、月饼……又甜又香,
煎有馓子、麻花、糖枣……又脆又爽,
自产自销各式糕点糖果,
深得顾客的青睐和赞扬。

桑家老二协助父母管理店面和财务,
老三带领两个外甥制作糕点负责烤炉,
李生抛弃妻儿执意跑上海,
女儿带着两个儿子靠娘家找活路。

老大一家五口分开单过,
住在隔壁另砌炉灶另起伙,
贴烧饼,煎油条,轧面条,

不论寒暑每天早市，生意很红火。

一年一度中秋节来临，
商家精心制作月饼新品，
椒盐、五仁、细沙……多种多样，
把甜蜜和吉庆呈献四乡八邻。

一个包一个品种，
一包足有两斤重，
桑周氏拎着一包包月饼，
战战兢兢走进何施两家家中。

何施两家是远近闻名的大财主，
占有小镇半条街的房产和店铺，
桑家就是向施家租用的店铺和住屋，
他们掌控着小镇的商贾。

桑周氏首先走进何家大堂，
"老爷、太太，新出炉的月饼请品尝！"
躺在躺椅上的何太太欠了欠身，
"有冬瓜月饼吗？我尝一尝！"

"这次没做这个品种，
我回去一定催着加工！"
何太太的一句话，
桑家不敢怠慢立马行动。

从买冬瓜到制馅做成月饼，
经过近十道工序才搞定，
第二天，桑周氏再次登门，
何太太咬了一口，连说"不行！不行！"

桑周氏灰头土脸回到家中，
原来冬瓜的水份不好掌控，
老三带领外甥立即动手从头再来，
步步小心边做边尝终获成功。

桑周氏露出多时不见的笑脸，
桑家的名气越传越响赞声一片，
掌柜积劳成疾一病不起撒手人寰，
桑周氏用弱小的肩膀扛起桑家一片天！

记忆中的桑义隆茶食店 / Sang Yilong snack store in memory

Chapter Two
Painstaking Efforts for Business

On the riverbank was the Shuangqiao Town under construction,
With the main east-west street two miles long.
There were shops for rice, cloth, meat, and drugs.
What was missing were those for tea snacks and cakes.

Should we stay here or continue eastward?
Nobody had any idea,
Son-in-law Li Sheng shook his head at the street,
"This little place is too shabby!"

In poor health, the boss frowned.
Mrs. Zhou-Sang put down her bound feet:
"Heaven sent us here,
Obeying God's will, we'll open a shop here!"

Sang Yilong's golden sign would stand undefeated
on the crossroads of the town for many years.
From then on, the tea snacks and pastries here,
Turned a new page and a new era.

For baked: crispy bread, cakes, moon cakes... sweet and aromatic; For fried: rice dumplings, twists, and candy dates... crispy and refreshing. Various self-made pastries and sweets won the favor and praise of customers.

The second son assisted parents to manage and do the finances. The third led his two nephews tending the pastries and the oven. Li Sheng headed on to Shanghai, abandoning his children and wife, who had to rely on her parents.

The eldest son and his family of five lived alone next door. Pasted sesame seed cakes, fried dough sticks, and noodles, They opened the store every morning, be it cold or hot,

And the business was booming.

The annual Mid-Autumn Festival was coming,
Merchants carefully made new mooncakes.
Salt and pepper, five nuts, fine bean paste...,
Presented sweetness and auspiciousness to neighbors.

One variety in each package, about one kilogram heavy.
Carrying bags of mooncakes,
Mrs. Zhou-Sang walked into He's and Shi's homes
with trepidation.

Being famously rich, the He and Shi families
possessed half of the street's properties and shops.
They controlled the merchants of the town.
From the Shi, the Sang rented the shop and house.

Mrs. Zhou-Sang first walked into the lobby of the He family.
"Sir, Madam, please try the newly baked mooncakes!"
Mrs. He, leaned over from her recliner,
"Are there any winter melon mooncakes? Let me try one!"

"We didn't make this variety this time.
I will tell them to when I get back! "
A word from Mrs. He, the Sang family didn't dare
to neglect and took action immediately.

From purchasing to making fillings to make mooncakes,
It took nearly ten steps to get done.
The next day, Zhou-Sang visited again.
Mrs. He took a bite and kept saying, "No! No!"

Mrs. Zhou-Sang returned home disgraced. It turned out
that the water in the winter melon was difficult to control.
The third son led his nephews to start all over again.
They took caution each step and finally succeeded.

Mrs. Zhou-Sang showed a smile which hadn't been seen for long, praises abounded with the spread of Sang's fame. The boss, unfortunately, fell ill due to overwork and passed away. Mrs. Zhou-Sang supported the family on weak shoulders!

小镇一角/A corner in town

第三章
何佬佬

"只进不出何佬佬,
哇啦哇啦杨三宝。"
小镇几代人的心里
都会想起这两句童谣。

何佬佬就是何财主的太太,
早晨的集市是她常去的所在,
她看上的东西拿了就走,
价钱多少、给不给,由她说由她宰。

一天何太太在集上逛店,
来到一位卖鸡蛋的农妇面前,
"把蛋送到我家里!"
她的话就是一道令箭。

农妇把蛋篮轻轻放在何家门前,
她习惯地伸手向何太太要钱,
何太太不理不睬拿起蛋篮走进家门,
农妇见状一把夺过蛋篮不顾情面。

何太太一个趔趄撞上了门框,
她回头扇了农妇一记耳光,
"混帐!不撒泡尿照照自己,
竟敢动手从我手里来抢!"

农妇忍气吞声回到自己的摊位上,
"不讲理,不给钱,还打人耳光!"
左右的乡邻们纷纷好言相劝:
"这种人惹不起,更不能顶撞!"

何太太怒气冲冲追来纠缠,
"睁开狗眼看看这是谁家的地盘!
让你站在这里不收你的钱,

已经是宽宏大量积德行善!"

她一眼看到了农夫脚前的蛋篮,
伸手一脚踢翻了鸡蛋。
看着满地的蛋壳和黄白相间的蛋液,
农妇气愤满腔泪湿衣衫。

"我爸正病倒在床上,
等我卖掉鸡蛋去抓药煎汤,
现在没有了唯一的财源,
我爸也失去了生的希望!"

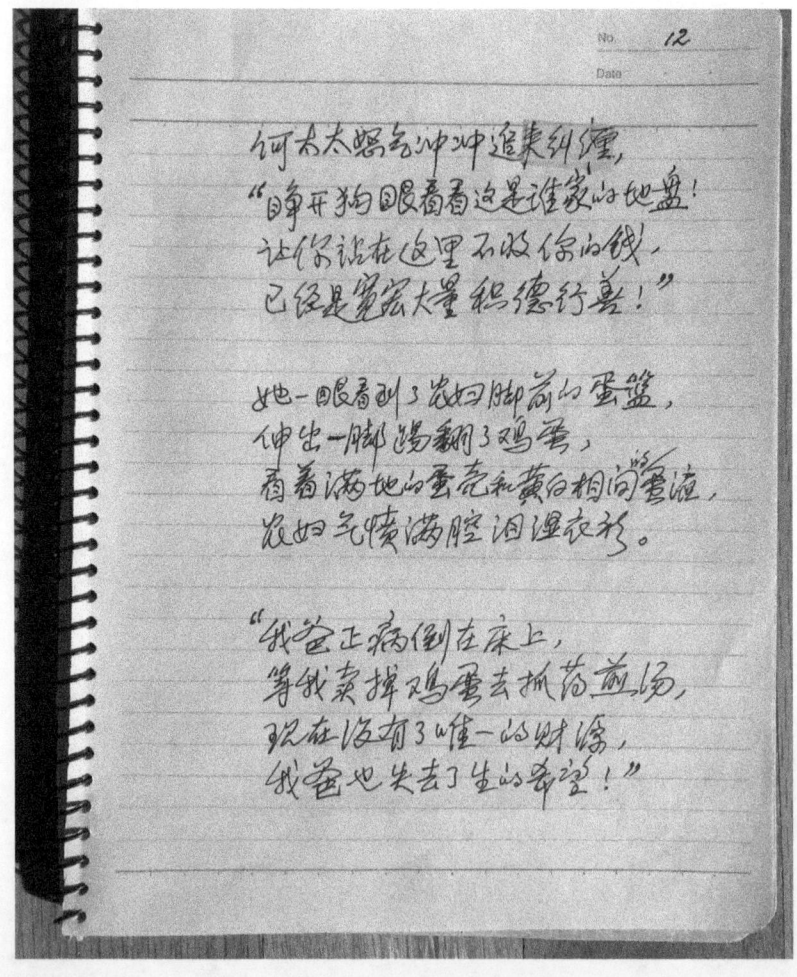

Chapter Three
He Laolao

"You can't get anything from He Laolao,
Blah blah uproars Yang Sanbao."
Generations in the small town
All knew well this nursery rhyme.

He Laolao was the wife of Mr. He,
The morning market was where she frequented.
She just took what she liked and left.
It was up to her how much and whether to pay at all.

One day Mrs. He was in the market.
She came to a peasant woman selling eggs,
"Send the eggs to my house!"
Her words were like an arrow of command.

Gently placed the egg basket in front of He's house,
The old woman habitually reached out to Mrs. He for money.
Mrs. He picked up the basket and walked in.
Seeing this, the peasant grabbed the basket without thinking.

Mrs. He stumbled and hit the door frame.
She turned around and slapped the peasant in the face.
"Damn it! Didn't you pee and take a look at yourself in it?
How dare you rob me!"

The peasant woman swallowed anger and returned to her stall.
"Unreasonable, not paying, instead, slapping me!"
The neighbors around offered sympathy and advice: "You can't
offend this kind of person, let alone collide with her!"

Mrs. He chased her back angrily.
"Open your dog eyes and see whose territory this is!
By letting you stand here for free,

I am already magnanimous and charitable!"

Seeing the egg basket in front of the peasant's feet,
She kicked the basket over. Looking at the shells
and yellow and white liquid all over the ground,
The peasant was so angry her clothes were soaked with tears.

"My dad is lying ill in bed,
Waiting for me to sell the eggs to get some medicine.
Now the only source of income is gone,
My dad's also lost his hope of living!"

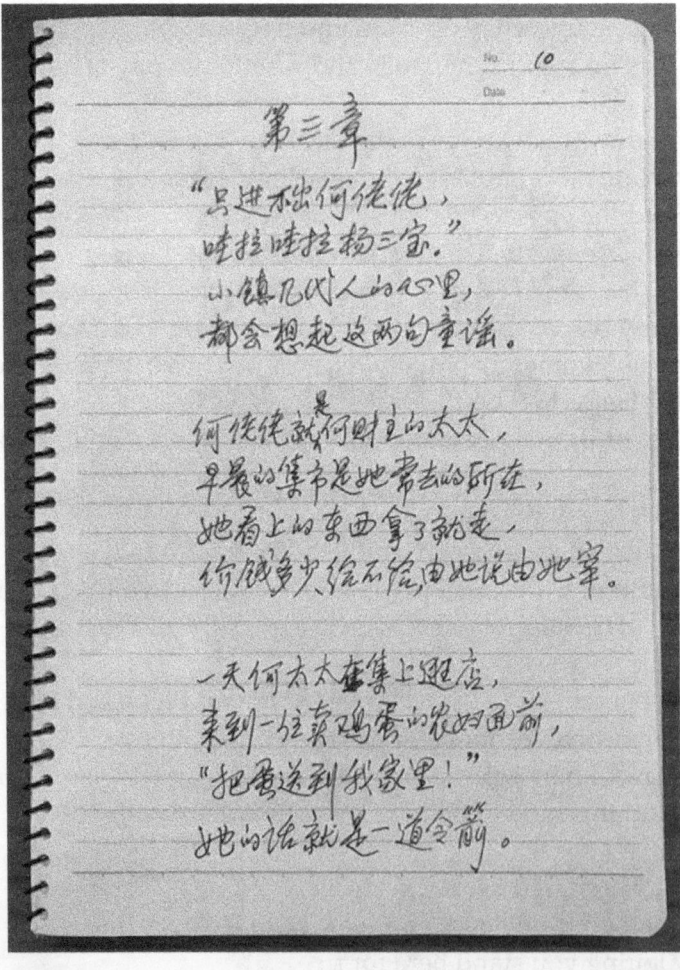

第四章
杨三宝

第一节
小石狗

杨三宝是乡公所的一个保镖,
整天围着乡长的屁股跑,
派苛捐、征杂税、抓壮丁,无恶不作,
镇里镇外随时都能听到他的咆哮。

一天上午乡公所门外吵吵闹闹,
杨三宝挥舞棍棒大声吼叫:
"你小子胆子不小竟敢开小差,
我打断你腿看你还跑不跑?"

这逃兵是镇上一个无业游民,
大家叫他小石狗,他没有大名,
父亲因病早早过世,
家里只有母子俩相依为命。

他帮店铺挑水打杂,
挣点血汗钱养活妈妈;
妈妈一手拗篮一手撑根竹竿,
走乡串户上门乞讨挨打挨骂。

一天妈妈病得不能动弹,
家里没米下锅煮饭,
像热锅上的蚂蚁
小石狗急得跳脚一筹莫展。

他曾听到镇上有人议论,
有钱人可以出钱买壮丁;
小石狗忽然灵机一动,
决定卖壮丁养活母亲。

有人求之不得交易立马成功,
小石狗高高兴兴把钱送到母亲手中;
妈妈哭天抹泪难舍难分,
抱着儿子久久不放松。

国军不是征粮就是拉夫欺压百姓,
小石狗人在兵营心在家庭;
一天部队开拔远走他乡,
他假装伤病偷偷逃出兵营。

小石狗刚刚迈进家门,
杨三宝一眼看到了他的身影;
母子相见嘘寒问暖泪水涟涟,
杨三宝闯门抓住了小石狗的衣领。

围观群众看不下去纷纷说情:
"放开他吧,太可怜了,母子情深!"
小石狗最终被押回了兵营,
母亲在家贫病交加孤苦伶仃。

第二节
绑票

"柝!柝!柝!"三响梆子声,
"火烛小心,夜夜当心!"
更夫老张头走过静静的街头,
十多个黑影突然闯入了人们的梦境。

敲门、撞门,吆喝、哭闹,
整个小镇鸡飞狗跳鬼哭狼嚎,
商家店铺惨遭洗劫,
还有十二个人被匪徒绑票。

桑家老少睡眼惺忪挤在一旁,
三名匪徒凶神恶煞持刀弄枪,

"怎么只有这一点儿钱?
当家的跟我们走一趟!"

"妈妈年事已高身体不好,
店里生意清淡萧条。"
老二站了出来被匪徒带走,
一家人提心吊胆再也睡不着觉。

小镇被噩梦笼罩,
店铺关门,街道冷清,行人稀少,
家里忙着筹钱筹粮,
尽快救出亲人免遭匪徒撕票。

桑义隆是受害的商家之一,
老二被绑票只得关门歇业;
为了让老二尽快回家开店,
全家凑齐并交去了十担[1]大米。

杨三宝一天酒后吐了真言:
"他们总是拖欠捐税太久,
不买我的帐,我给他们颜色看,
这就叫敬酒不吃吃罚酒!"

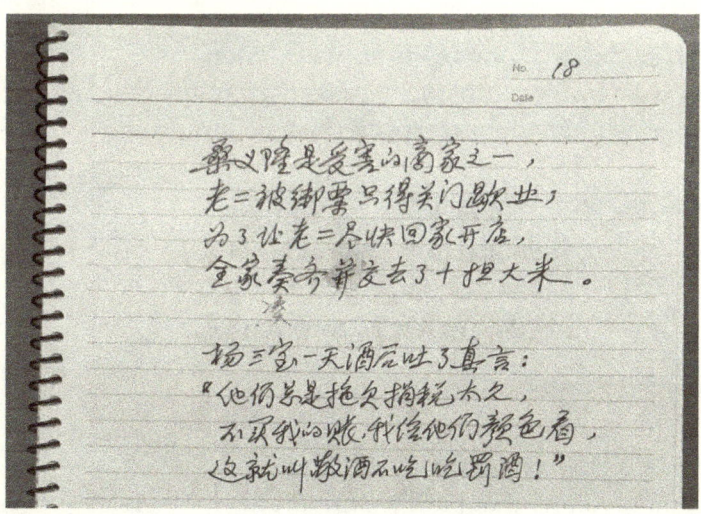

1 一担为50公斤

Chapter Four
Yang Sanbao

i. Little Stone Dog

A bodyguard at the township office, Yang Sanbao ran around the mayor's ass all day long. He levied miscellaneous taxes, forced young men to be soldiers, and did all kinds of evil. His roar could be heard at any time in and out of town.

One morning there was a lot of noise outside
the township office. Yang Sanbao waved his stick
and shouted loudly: "You are so audacious you dared to desert,
I'll break your legs to see if you can still run!"

This deserter was a jobless man in the town.
Everyone called him Little Stone Dog, as he had no real name.
His father passed away young due to illness.
Only his mother depended on him in the family.

He carried water and did odd jobs for shops
To earn some sweat money to support mom;
Mom held a basket with one hand and a bamboo pole with
the other, walking door to door to beg, be beaten and scolded.

One day his mother was too sick to move.
They didn't have any food at home.
Like an ant on a hot pot, Little Stone Dog was anxious,
But there was nothing he could do.

He recalled people talking in town
About rich people paying others to join the army for them;
Little Stone Dog suddenly had an idea,
Deciding to follow that path to support his mother.

Some was just looking for that offer.
Little Stone Dog happily handed the money to his mother;
Crying her tears, unable to part,
Mom held her son for a long time.

The national army either requisitioned food
or oppressed the people. Little Stone Dog's mind dwelled
about home; One day the troops left for a foreign place,
He pretended injury and fled the barracks.

The moment he entered the house,
Yang Sanbao happened to see him;
When mom and son met, their tears poured out.
Yang broke in and grabbed the kid by the collar.

The onlookers all expressed their condolences:
"Let him go, poor mother and son!"
Little Stone Dog was finally escorted back to the barracks.
The mom stayed at home, sick and all alone.

ii. The Kidnap

"Twuh! Twuh! Twuh!" Three bangs sounded.
"Watch out for fire, be careful!" The old watchman Lao Zhang
walked through the quiet streets. Over a dozen black shadows
suddenly broke into people's dreams.

Knocking, banging, shouting, crying,
Chickens fluttering, dogs barking, the town fell into chaos.
Merchants and shops were looted.
Over twelve people were kidnapped.

The Sang family huddled aside sleepily.
Three gangsters viciously waved knives and guns.
"Only this little money?
Who's in charge? Come with us!"

"My mother is old and in poor health.
Business has been slow and sluggish."
The second son stood up and was taken away.
The family could never go back to sleep again.

The town shrouded in nightmare, shops closed,
Streets deserted, and few pedestrians were seen.
The Sangs were busy raising money,
To rescue the son from the gangsters.

The son of Sang Yilong was kidnapped,
So they had to close down business;
In order for him to come back and resume business,
The family gathered and handed over ten stones of rice.[1]

Yang Sanbao blurted out the truth after drinking one day:
"They're always late on their taxes.
So I showed them the color.
They have to learn it the hard way!"

---

1 One stone=50 Kilograms

第五章
小镇姑娘

第一节
娟娟

小镇风水养人美女如云,
不同的选择带来了不同的命运,
这里有笑声,有眼泪,也有抗争,
每家都有一本精彩和难念的经。

桑老大生有三个"千金",
一个比一个聪明、漂亮;
经过他家门前的路人,
都会一次次回头张望。

大姐娟娟轻言慢语温柔善良,
人如其名端庄秀丽。
媒婆踏破了她家的门槛,
她就是不点头不答理。

妈妈懂得女儿的心,
娟娟早把小王当作了心上人。
小王两年前从苏北到这里做裁缝,
态度和蔼,手艺高超,赢得大家好评。

一手拿尺,一手握剪,左右逢源,
缝缝连连一手好针线,
娟娟呆呆地看着目不转睛,
心中的敬佩变成了爱恋。

她渐渐成了王师傅的帮手,
整理布料、线脑和针头;
王师傅手把手地教耐心细致,
她开始一针一线地缝制纽扣。

他裁她缝，他缝她纫，
两人从师徒渐渐成了情侣；
老大夫妇看在眼里心里也欢喜，
自由恋爱、自主婚姻成了小镇的先例。

第二节
冯家姐妹

冯家鞋铺和桑家隔街相望，
一双双鞋底鞋帮摆满了半个殿堂；
冯师傅手艺一流绱鞋又快又好，
姑娘少妇常向他投去钦羡的目光。

冯家两女儿是一对美丽的姐妹花，
大姐早定了娃娃亲有了婆家，
如今到了谈婚论嫁的时候，
大姐却大吵大闹变了卦。

"小时候订的亲不能算数！"
"收了用了男方彩礼没法向外吐！"
"谁收了用了彩礼谁嫁过去！"
"浑话！这个家这婚事我做主！"

父女俩日夜争吵没有结果，
大姐几次站在桥边要跳河，
妈妈劝劝女儿说说丈夫，
一家鸡犬不宁没有出路。

小妹看在眼里急在心里，
不忍爸爸和姐姐处在两难境地；
男大当婚，女大当嫁，
她挺身而出把姐姐顶替！

顿时冯家雨过天晴，
小镇众口称赞这对姐妹情深；

妹妹代替姐姐走进了婚姻殿堂，
大姐决心寻找自己的爱情。

大姐勇敢地跑到苏北解放区，
全身心地投入革命参加了解放战争，
后来担任了一个乡的妇联主任，
也找到了情投意合的心上人。

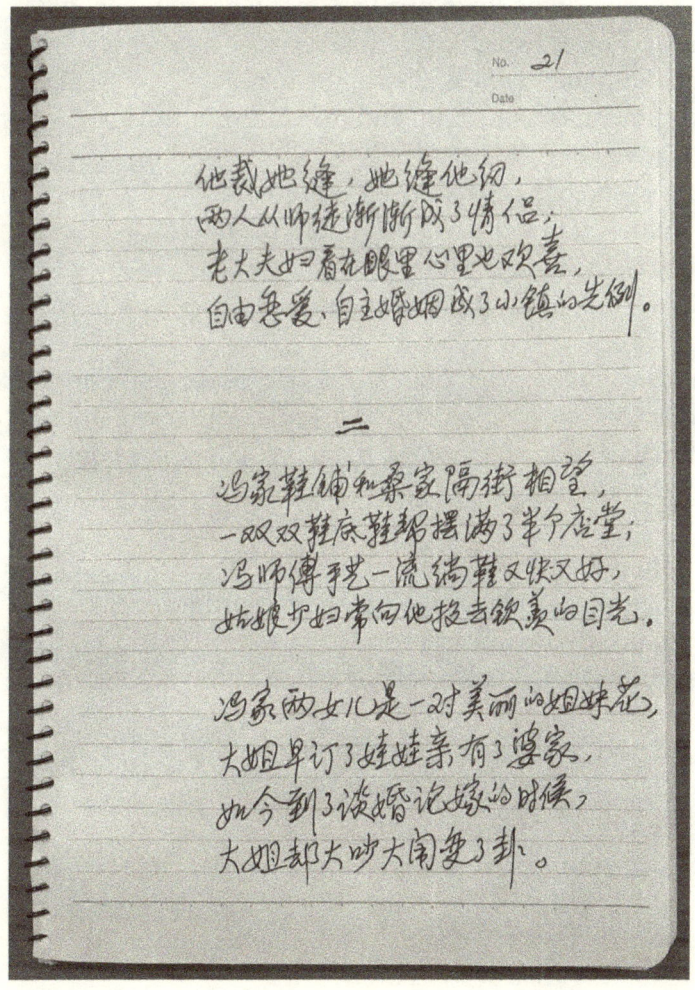

Chapter Five
Girls in the Town

i. Juanjuan

The feng shui of the town nurtures many beautiful people.
Different choices bring different fates.
There is laughter, tears, and struggle here.
Every family has wonderful and difficult scriptures.

The eldest son of Sang had three daughters,
Each smarter and more beautiful than the other;
People passing by his house,
Would all look back again and again.

The eldest daughter Juanjuan was soft-spoken, gentle and kind.
The look was as dignified and beautiful as her name suggested.
Matchmakers almost flattened the threshold of her home.
She just wouldn't nod or agree.

Her mom understood Juanjuan had long regarded Xiao Wang
as her sweetheart, who came here from northern Jiangsu
to be a tailor two years ago.
His kindness and superb craftsmanship had won everyone.

A ruler in one hand and scissors in the other,
Sewing a good needle and thread.
Juanjuan stared at him admiringly,
Which turned into love in her heart.

She gradually became Master Wang's helper,
Arranging fabrics, threads, and needles;
Wang taught patiently and meticulously.
She began sewing the buttons stitch by stitch.

One tailoring and the other sewing,
They changed from master and apprentice to lovers;
The parents saw it and were also happy.
Free love and marriage precedented the small town.

ii. Feng's Girls

Feng's shoe shop and Sang's shop were across the street.
Pairs of soles and uppers filled half the store;
Master Feng's shoes were made quickly and well.
Girls and young women often cast admiring glances at him.

The two Feng daughters were beautiful.
The elder's marriage had long been arranged in her youth.
Now it was time to carry it out,
She made a fuss and refused to.

The marriage you decided for me doesn't count!"
"I can't spit it out after I received the bride gift from the man!"
"Whoever accepted it shall marry him!"
"Nonsense! I have the final say about the marriage!"

The father and daughter quarreled day and night to no avail.
The daughter stood by the bridge several times and wanted
to jump into the river. The mother talked to both of them.
But there was no way out for this family.

Being also anxious in her heart,
The younger sister couldn't bear that dilemma.
A person should get married at a certain age.
She stepped forward to replace her sister!

Suddenly the sky cleared up in the Feng family.
Everyone in the town praised the sisters for their deep affections.
The younger tied the knot for the older sister,
The latter was determined to find her own love.

She bravely ran to the Northern Jiangsu liberated area,
Devoting herself wholeheartedly to the revolution.
Later, she served as the director of the Women's
Federation of a township, and also found her sweetheart.

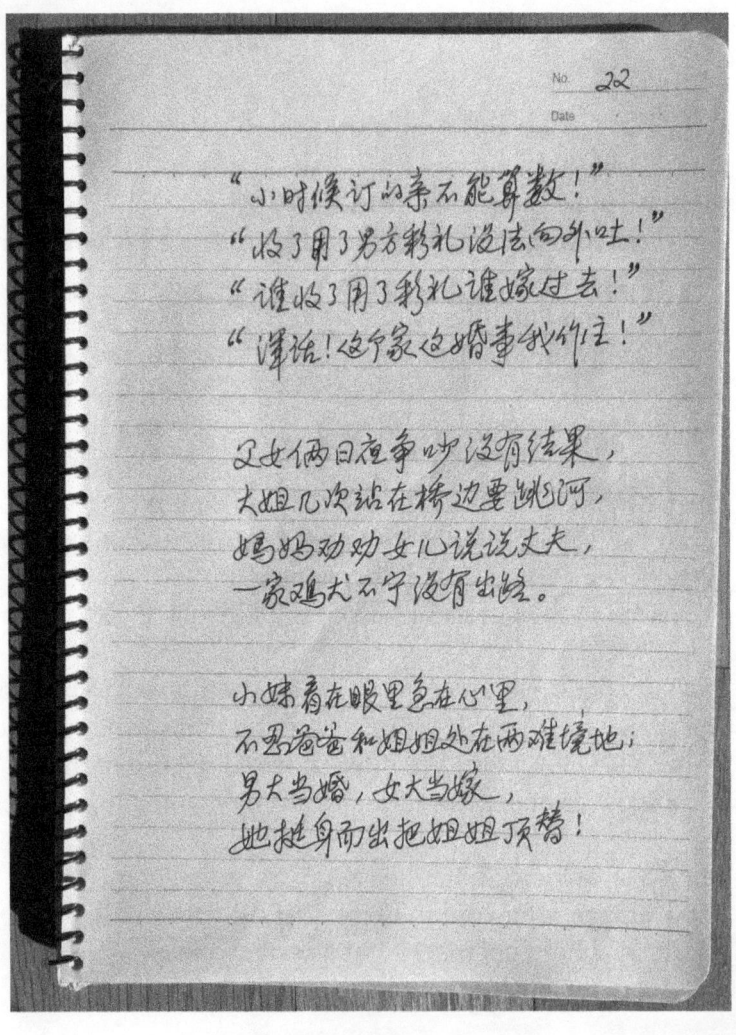

第六章
小镇肉铺

小镇一时风云突变,
人的祸福也难预料;
"东洋人上岸啦!"
镇北茅家娘子发出了凄厉的呼叫。

目睹了日寇杀人、奸淫的兽行,
茅娘子受到惊吓得了神经病,
她不分昼夜边走边喊"东洋人上岸了!"
似乎在唤醒睡梦中的乡邻。

连接东西街的大桥桥堍头,
一对小夫妻经营着一家肉铺,
老板娘娇小玲珑标致妩媚,
老板矮小结实人称许师傅。

许师傅剁肉称肉手脚不停,
一刀下去一称一个准;
老板娘翘着兰花指数钱找钱,
令人眼花缭乱头发晕。

肉铺每天顾客盈门,
有的真买肉有的是观景:
一是欣赏许师傅的"一刀准",
二是看老板娘的手巧心灵。

一天,肉铺老板娘外出讨债,
远远看到一小队日本兵走来,
她立即闪进路边的乱坟场,
平时怕鬼现在更怕魔怪。

身上蚂蚁爬扰蚊虫叮咬,
头顶苍蝇飞舞炎阳高照,
厄运突然降临鬼子扑了过来,

眼前一黑头脑空白遭到了强暴。

从此她失去了娇美的容颜，
也没有了往日的笑谈，
她心里的天已经坍塌破碎，
永远失去了上天赋予她做母亲的神圣头衔！

几天后，一个鬼子撞上门来，
许师傅用酒肉招待，
这天，肉铺关门停止营业，
那个鬼子再也没见出来。

第二天公鸡开始第一次啼叫，
肉铺正常营业开门很早，
许师傅挥刀剁肉又快又准，
老板娘脸上浮现了一丝欣慰的微笑。

Chapter Six
The Butcher Shop

The small town suddenly changed weather.
It was also difficult to predict people's fates;
"The Japs are ashore!"
Mrs. Mao of the northern town shrieked a mournful scream.

Having witnessed the invaders' brutal murder and rape,
Mrs. Mao was scared into mental chaos.
She walked around day and night, shouting, "The Japs
are ashore!" as if to wake up the sleeping neighbors.

Off to the bridge connecting East and West streets,
A young couple ran a butcher shop.
The landlady was petite, exquisite, and charming.
The boss, short and stocky, was called Master Xu.

Xu chopped and weighed meat,
Accurately getting how much you needed.
With her orchid-like fingers, the landlady counted money.
Everything was dazzling and made you dizzy.

The shop was packed every day.
Some came for meat and others just watched:
Either to appreciate Master Xu's precision,
Or to see the dexterity of the landlady.

One day, the proprietress went out to collect debts,
When she saw a small group of Japanese soldiers approaching.
She immediately ducked into a cemetery on the roadside,
Usually fearing ghosts, now even more afraid of monsters.

Ants crawled and mosquitos bit.
Flies buzzed overhead with the sun shining.
Misfortune suddenly struck when the Japs pounced.

Her eyes black, her mind blank, she was raped.

Thence, she lost her beautiful look,
No more smiles and chit-chats.
The sky in her heart had collapsed broken.
She was deprived forever of the sacred title of mother!

Several days later, a Jap dropped in.
Master Xu entertained him with wine and meat.
That day, the butcher shop was closed for business.
The Japanese was never seen again.

The next day the rooster boasted the first crow,
When the butcher shop opened its door.
Master Xu chopped meat quickly and accurately.
A smile of relief appeared on the face of the landlady.

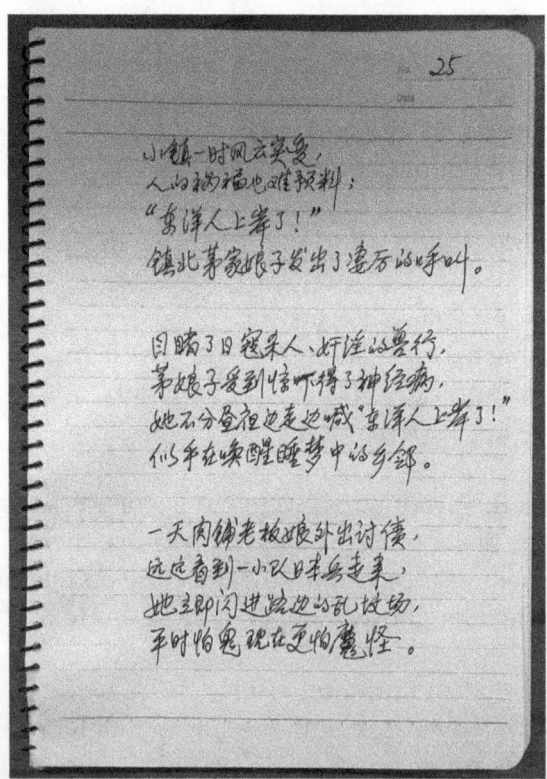

第七章
新春劫难

第一节
辞旧迎新

进入腊月人们忙着迎接新春，
商家店铺制作销售年货忙个不停；
大多买鱼买肉蒸糕蒸馒头，
敬神祭祖隆重又虔诚。

腊月二十四小年临近新年门槛，
家家祭灶清新神龛，
供的是一碗赤豆米饭一碗豆腐青菜，
祈愿灶神赤诚为民一清二白！

"上天言好事，
下界保平安。"
神龛上的这幅对联，
出自平民百姓的心坎！

桑家祭祖设在后院堂屋，
两扇大门上的对联特别醒目：
上联"风调雨顺"，下联"国泰民安"，
为本镇清末秀才黄桐先生新书。

长条桌上祭品摆满，
正中放着猪头一盘，
上面批挂红纸条，
预示来年生意红火有个好的开端。

一条大鱼头翘尾翘，
余来余去家庭富饶，
全家老少向祖先顶礼膜拜，
一脸严肃面向祖先静悄悄。

小镇西街关帝庙紫气飘渺,
东街城隍庙香烟缭绕,
炮竹声声辞旧迎新,
祈望全镇来年繁荣昌盛热热闹闹。

第二节
二次劫难

零乱的枪击声击碎了小镇的安宁,
这里又遭到了第二次厄运,
国民党军队兵败如山倒,
把灾难带给了无辜的百姓。

如果说上次土匪抢劫绑票,
犹如几个蚱蜢蹦达,
这次则是成群的蝗虫,
飞临小镇把百姓糟蹋。

各家各户准备好的年货,
整锅整碗的鸡鸭鱼肉,
瞬间不翼而飞点滴不剩,
统统进入狼肚虎口。

清晨家人从噩梦中醒来,
面对空空的橱柜和破碎的锅碗,
似乎又回到了可怖的梦境,
面临一个又一个灾难。

上午在崇实中学的大操场上,
南通县县长向民众发表演讲:
"弟兄们几天几夜粒米未沾,
更没有鱼肉的美味可尝!"

明目张胆抢劫掠夺,
花言巧语辩解开脱,

官府和国军一个鼻孔出气，
全然不顾老百姓的死活！

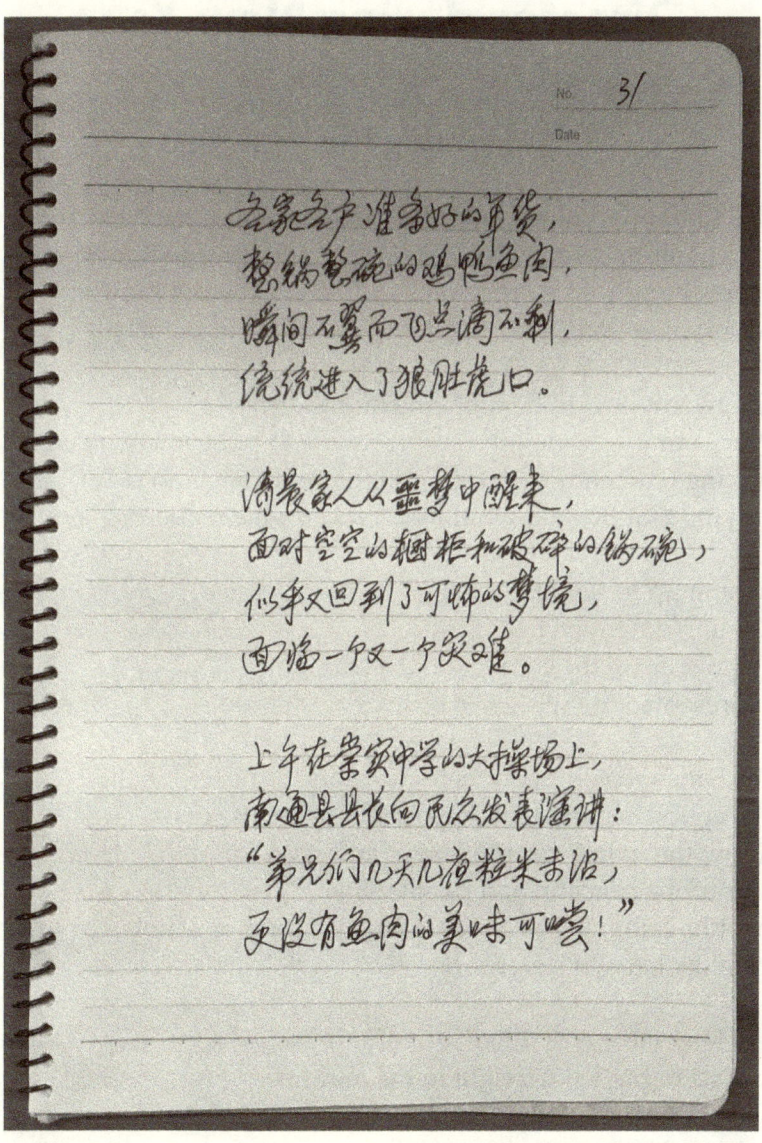

Chapter VII
Disaster during New Year

i. Welcoming the New Year

The 12th lunar month saw all busy welcoming the New Year.
Merchants and shops were making and selling festive goods;
People bought fish, meat, and steamed cakes and buns,
Worshiping gods and ancestors solemnly and piously.

The twenty-fourth day into the month,
Every family cleaned the shrine to worship the kitchen god,
Serving red beans with rice, and tofu with vegetables,
Praying that the god would sincerely do them good!

"Going up to say nice things,
Coming down to bless us safe."
The words on the couplet on the shrine,
Represented the wishes of ordinary mankind!

The Sangs worshipped their ancestors in the back hall,
The couplets particularly eye-catching on the door:
"May the wind be moderate and rain smooth," "May the country be peaceful and people safe,"
Freshly calligraphed by Mr. Huang Tong, a scholar in town from the late Qing Dynasty.

The long table was filled with offerings,
A plate of pig's head right in the middle.
Red papers hanging on it,
Indicated a good start for business next year.

A big fish with its head and tail raised,
Symbolized the household would be rich.
The whole family, young and old,

Bowed to their ancestors quietly and solemnly.

The Guandi Temple on West had a misty purple atmosphere.
The Chenghuang Temple on East was filled with incense smoke.
The firecrackers bid farewell to the old and welcomed the new,
Wishing the town prosperous and lively in the coming year.

ii. The Second Disaster

Scattered gunshots shattered the tranquility of the town.
Here came the second misfortune.
The Kuomintang army was defeated like a falling mountain,
Bringing disaster to innocent masses.

If the last time the bandits that robbed and kidnapped people,
Were like a few grasshoppers hopping,
This time it was like swarms of locusts,
Flying into small towns to ruin humanity.

The New Year's goods every household had prepared—
Whole pots and bowls of chicken, duck, and fish,
Gone in an instant and not a drop left,
All entered the wolf's belly and the tiger's mouth.

After sunrise, families woke up from a nightmare,
Facing the empty cupboards and broken pots and pans,
As if they had returned to the terrible dream,
Encountering one disaster after another.

In the morning on the playground of Chongshi Middle School,
The magistrate of Nantong County delivered a speech:
"Our army buddies haven't had a grain of rice for days,
Not to mention delicious fish and meat!"

Towards blatant robbery and plunder, using sugary words
to excuse themselves, the government and the national army

breathed through the same nose,
Completely disregarding the life or death of the populace!

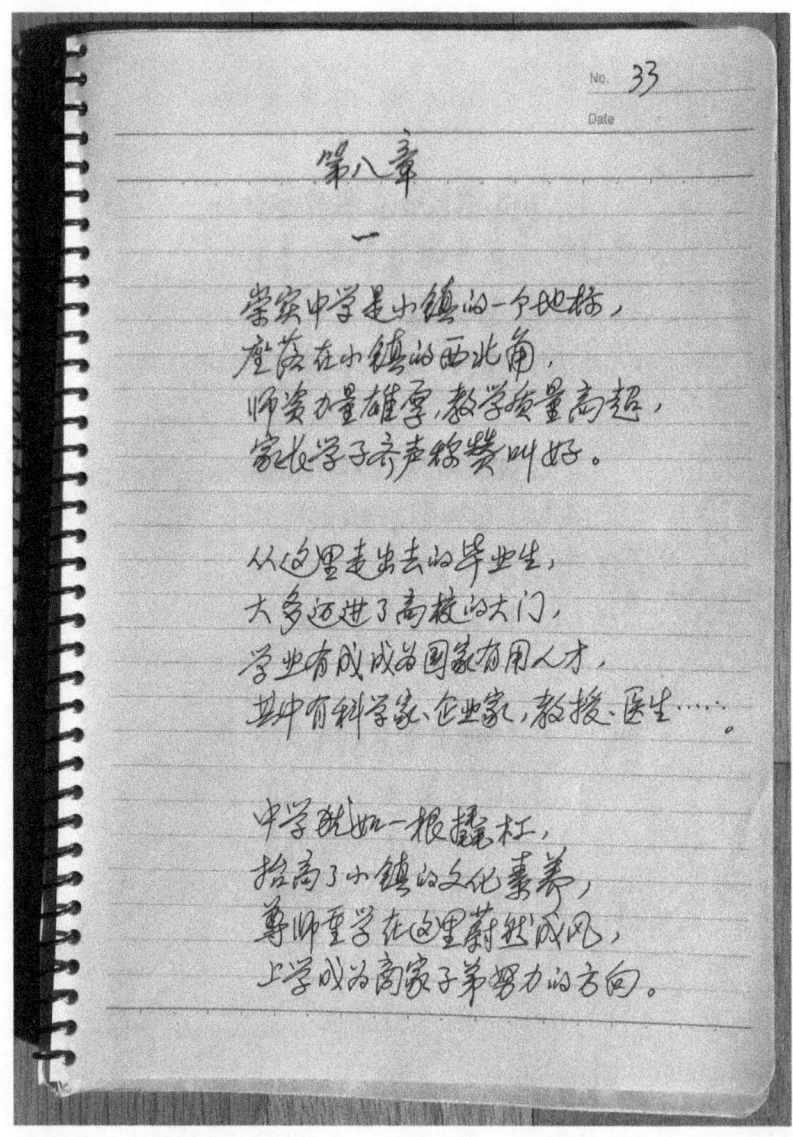

第八章
崇实中学

第一节
嫁教师

崇实中学是小镇的一个地标,
座落在小镇的西北角,
师资力量雄厚,教学质量高超,
家长学子齐声称赞叫好。

从这里走出去的毕业生,
大多迈进了高校的大门,
学业有成成为国家有用人才,
其中有科学家、企业家、教授、医生……。

中学犹如一根撬杠,
抬高了小镇的文化素养,
尊师重学在这里蔚然成风,
上学成为商家子弟努力的方向。

中学教师走在街道上,
迎来的都是尊敬和爱慕的目光,
更有年轻姑娘大言不惭,
"非教师不嫁"的话流传很广。

镇西一位姓蒋的姑娘,
父母为她订亲物色了对象,
她一次次地把男方彩礼扔出门外,
早把中学袁老师放在了心上。

南市梢施家三姐,
年过三十还深闺在家,
父母亲又急又气,
她坚守自己的信念:"不爱的不嫁!"

中学走来了一位张先生,
中等身材貌不出众,
说话慢条斯理,态度和蔼可亲,
一眼就被三姐看中。

施家三姐终于嫁人完婚,
成了小镇的一大新闻,
老姑娘和中学教师的结合,
为这里的婚姻植入了文化之根。

第二节
学生事故

小镇中学名声远扬,
不少学生来自外县他乡,
远离数百公里外的盐城,
也有学生慕名到这里上学堂。

江南江北不同的气候和环境,
北来的学生难以适应,
第一个寒假还没有正式开始,
他们急匆匆赶紧回家探亲。

不料那天寒潮来袭,
船在江面没处没法躲避,
狂风巨浪掀翻了船只,
旅客纷纷落水危在旦夕。

当时多方全力施助抢救,
七名崇中学生溺水冻僵把命丢,
陈校长引咎自责急火攻心,
愧病交加在虞山脚下长眠不朽。

Chapter Eight
Chongshi Middle School

i. Marrying a Teacher

Located in the northwest of the town as a landmark,
Chongshi Middle School had a strong faculty.
For the excellent teaching quality,
Parents and students praised her in unison.

Most of her graduates enter colleges or universities,
Succeeding in their studies.
Growing into useful talents for the country,
They are scientists, entrepreneurs, professors, doctors...

Like a crowbar, the school raised the literacy of the town.
Respecting teachers and valuing learning,
Is a common practice here.
Going to school has become the business children's goal.

Walking on the street,
The teachers were greeted with respect and admiration.
There were even bolder young girls,
Who claimed they wouldn't marry unless to a teacher.

This girl named Jiang in the west of the town,
Whose parents found a guy for her,
She threw the man's bride gifts out of the door once and again,
As she had long had the school teacher Yuan in her heart.

The third sister of Shi's family in the south,
Over thirty and still living in a boudoir at home.
Her parents were anxious and angry.
Yet she stuck to her belief: "Won't marry anyone I don't love!"

Teacher Zhang was of medium height
and looked common.
He spoke slowly with an affable demeanor,
Who appealed to the third sister.

The third sister of the Shi family finally got married,
Which became big news in the town.
The combination of an old girl and a middle school teacher,
Planted cultural roots for marriage here.

ii. A Student Accident

The middle school enjoyed a reputation far and wide;
Many students came from outside the town,
Far as Yancheng, hundreds of kilometers away,
There were students from there who came for this school.

With different climates and environments in the south and north
of the Yangtze, it was difficult for the northerners to adapt.
The first winter vacation had not officially started yet,
Before they hurried home to visit family.

Unexpectedly, a cold wave hit that day.
The boat had nowhere to hide on the river.
It was overturned by the strong wind and waves. Passengers
fell into the water one after another and were in danger.

Many people tried their best to come to rescue.
Still seven Chongshi students drowned or froze to death.
President Chen blamed himself with guilt.
He fell ill and rested forever at the foot of Yushan Mountain.

第九章
兰兰和珍珍

第一节
兰兰

西街有一家制售馒头、烧饼的早点铺,
店主是拥有一双儿女的陆师傅,
妻子经常装神弄鬼为人除邪祛灾,
女儿兰兰快嘴快舌咋咋呼呼。

一天城隍庙前乱纷纷,
杨三宝拷问"小偷"手辣心狠,
兰兰挤进人群大吼一声:
杨三宝!放开他,他还是一个小囡!"

听到愤激的声音不禁一愣,
杨三宝很少遇到有人在他面前打横,
一看是怒气冲冲的兰兰,
他立马收敛言行不再闹腾。

杨三宝对兰兰早已垂涎,
有事没事有话没话总想见她一面,
但是兰兰就是不看不理不睬,
这次让他似乎看到了希望一线。

他放开了那个小孩不再动粗,
嬉皮笑脸辩解"那只是吓唬吓唬!"
他趁机凑到兰兰的面前,
嘴脸完全变成了另外一副。

他以为兰兰回心转意向他低头,
急不可耐就要抓她的手,
兰兰一下甩开了他的魔爪,
飞快地从他的身边逃走。

杨三宝拔脚就追加快脚步,
一把抓住了兰兰的胳膊不放;
兰兰拼命挣扎扬起右手,
狠狠扇了杨三宝一记响亮的耳光。

望着远去的兰兰背影,
杨三宝气得咬牙发抖,
"你躲得了初一,躲不了十五,
总有一天把你弄到手!"

兰兰对自己的婚事自有主意,
不听媒妁之言不顾父母着急;
驻军周连长向她承诺:
尽快离开军队同她结为连理。

解放战争的枪炮声越来越近,
国民党的军队末日来临;
周连长识时务举白旗向解放军投诚,
最后获准回到小镇同兰兰成亲。

第二节
珍珍

薛季港位于镇南一里处,
港西是小学,港东是坟场埋有累累白骨,
双桥小学是小镇的又一文化标志,
镇上学业有成者大多从这里起步。

樊校长全力以赴白手起校,
从砌教室、购课桌到任教;
由初小完小发展为中心小学,
是十里八乡孩子们上学的首选目标。

小学位于乡镇的中心地带,
见证了新旧社会的不同时代,

旧政府在这里征钱粮、抓壮丁，欺压百姓，
新社会在这里斗地主、分田地，人民笑逐颜开。

种瓜得瓜，种豆得豆，
批斗会上何佬佬向那位农妇认罪低头；
杨三宝等不法分子得到应有的惩处，
关的关，毙的毙，一个也不漏。

还有少数地主、反革命分子逃避外头，
何财主家二儿子认清形势向政府自首，
他带领公安人员到上海追捕，
把他们一一捉拿监收。

一天这里召开群众大会进行公审，
劳苦大众欢欣鼓舞庆祝翻身做主人，
控诉罪恶滔天的旧社会，
向罪大恶极的地主反革命分子报仇雪恨。

小镇西街吴姓地主丧心病狂，
资助并组织反革命武装对抗解放，
工作队王队长代表人民政府宣读判决书，
这名反革命分子被押赴了刑场。

王队长常熟人参加革命多年，
视人民群众为亲人，对敌人不讲情面，
为了革命工作耽误了青春和爱情，
但又是革命工作为他牵上了红线。

这根红线的另一头握在珍珍手中，
桑老大的二女儿珍珍才貌出众，
她以自己的大姐娟娟为榜样，
找到了心上人，同王队长心心相印、相通。

兰兰和珍珍的不同选择，
给她们的命运带来美好和曲折，
一个在城里生活顺山顺水，
一个在乡下务农一生坎坷。

Chapter Nine
Lanlan and Zhenzhen

i. Lanlan

There was a breakfast shop on West Street.
The owner, Master Lu, had a son and a daughter.
His wife, an exorcist, warded off evil spirits.
Daughter Lanlan was talkative and righteous.

One day there was chaos in front of the Town Temple.
Yang Sanbao tortured the "thief" ruthlessly.
Lanlan squeezed into the crowd and shouted:
"Yang Sanbao! Let him go, he is just a child!"

Stunned when hearing the angry voice,
Yang rarely had people confronting him.
Seeing it was angry Lanlan,
He immediately restrained himself.

Having been long coveted Lanlan,
Yang Sanbao always wanted her company,
Although Lanlan just ignored him.
This time he seemed to see a glimmer of hope.

He let go of the child, and defended himself
with a playful smile, "That was just a bluff!"
He took the opportunity to get close to Lanlan,
With a totally different face.

Thinking Lanlan had changed her mind,
He impatiently tried to grab her hand.
Lanlan disgustedly shook off his claws,
And ran away without hesitation.

Quickening his pace to chase her,
Yang grabbed Lanlan's arm and wouldn't let go;
Struggling, Lanlan raised her right hand.
She slapped Yang Sanbao aloud in the face.

Watching her leave from behind,
Yang Sanbao gritted his teeth and trembled.
"You can escape today, but can't forever.
I'll definitely get you one day!"

Lanlan had her own ideas about her marriage.
Wouldn't listen to the matchmaker, ignored parents' worries.
Commander Zhou of the garrison promised her
To leave the army as soon as possible to marry her.

The gunfire of the Liberation was closer and closer,
So was the end of the Kuomintang.
Zhou surrendered to the Liberation army. Finally,
he was allowed to return to the small town to marry Lanlan.

ii. Zhenzhen

Xueji Harbor is located one mile south of the town.
To the west is a primary school, and east a cemetery.
Shuangqiao Primary School is another cultural symbol.
Most of the academically successful in the town started here.

Principal Fan went all out to build the school from scratch,
From building classrooms, purchasing desks to teaching;
It had developed from a junior primary to a central one,
The first school choice for children from all around.

Located in the center of the town, the primary school witnessed the different eras. The old government levied taxes, grabbed young men into army, oppressed people. The new society fought landlords, handed out fields, and people were happy.

You reap what you sow,
Mrs. He apologized to the peasant woman.
Yang Sanbao etc. were punished as they deserved,
Some imprisoned, others executed, not even one missed.

Still a few landlords and counter-revolutionaries were astray.
The second son of Mr. He's surrendered to the government.
He led the public security personnel to Shanghai,
The latter arrested the criminals one by one.

One day a mass meeting was held for a public trial.
The working people happily celebrated becoming masters,
Accusing the old society of crimes, taking revenge
on the heinous landlords and counter-revolutionaries.

The landowner Wu in the West Street funded and organized counter-revolutionary armed forces to fight against liberation. Captain Wang read out the verdict on behalf of the People's Government. Wu was taken to the execution ground.

Wang, from Changshu, had participated in the revolution for long. He treated the people as family and had no mercy towards the enemy. He put off love for revolutionary work. But it was his work that drew a red thread for him.

The other end of the thread was held in Zhenzhen's hand, Who was Sang's eldest son's second daughter, outstanding in talent and appearance. She took her eldest sister Juanjuan as an example, finding her love — Captain Wang.

Lanlan's and Zhenzhen's different choices,
Brought different beauty and destinies.
One lived smoothly in the city,
The other strenuously in the countryside.

第十章
游子归家

这天艳阳高照令人炫目,
喜鹊在枝头鸣叫飞舞,
十字街头李家来了一位不是客人的客人,
他就是十多年前独自闯荡上海的一家之主。

当年他抛弃妻儿去上海闯荡,
从此杳无音信迷失在十里洋场,
坑蒙拐骗沦为街头瘪三,
幸亏共产党拯救他才有了人样。

桑家大姐出生在传统的封建家庭,
从小缠绕裹脚为家命是听,
嫁鸡随鸡,嫁狗随狗,
丈夫李生鸡犬不如不管妻儿生死痛病。

大姐带着两个儿子无业无家,
只得投靠到娘家的屋檐下,
天天看着亲人但不是亲人的脸色,
寄人篱下十多个秋冬春夏。

好在有个经营茶食店的妈妈,
人能干,善良宽容,还很豁达,
中年丧夫一肩挑起了家庭和店铺,
把三儿一女一个个地拉扯长大。

大女儿一家的状况令她睡不着吃不香,
她像母鸡一样张开了温暖的翅膀,
力排他人的闲言碎语异见非议,
把女儿一家紧紧拢在自己的身旁。

不拖累娘家,不增加娘家负担,
女儿每天忙个不停没明没暗,
一针一线帮人家缝制衣衫裤袜,

把微薄的收入交给妈妈情愿心甘。

两个儿子早熟懂事不吃白饭，
外婆舅家杂七杂八的事务都抢着干，
制作茶食糕点，不管是油炸还是烧烤，
总是不怕苦，不怕累，不怕流汗。

天苍苍，地茫茫，
十多年时间说短不短说长不长，
两个儿子都过了谈婚成嫁的年纪，
大姐也让岁月铸成了老太婆的模样。

政府有关部门来信征询意见，
李生举目无亲没有落脚地点，
何去何从关系到他的后半生乃至晚年，
最好出路就是回到被拆散的家庭方不方便。

提到丈夫大姐恨得咬牙，
一去十多年眼里心里就没有她和伢，
不管妻子小脚伶仃行动不便，
不管两个儿子的抚养、教育，岁岁年年。

好在共产党领导得到了解放，
分得了土地分得了住房，
大儿子当上了供销社的经理，
小儿子练就好手艺工作在糕点作坊。

叶落归根，水归大海，
魂归故里即使终生在外；
他毕竟还是两个儿子的父亲，
"回家吧！"大姐敞开了宽大的胸怀！

终于大姐竖立起真正属于自己的门户
终于夫妻团圆父子相聚；
李生也最终回到了自己的家，
用忏悔洗刷灵魂迈出余生新的一步。

Chapter Ten
Strayed Soul Back

The sun was shining brightly,
Magpies chirping on the branches.
A guest yet not a guest came to the Li's. He was the head
of the family who had gone to Shanghai over a decade ago.

Back then, he abandoned his wife and children,
Never since been heard from as if having disappeared.
He had messed around with a street gang,
And was fortunately saved by the Communist Party.

Born into a traditional feudal family, the eldest daughter
of the Sang family was obedient and her feet bound.
Even if you marry a chicken, follow the chicken; a dog, follow
the dog. Worse still, Li didn't care about her or the kids.

Unemployed and homeless,
She and her two sons could only take refuge with her parents'.
Being cautious around their relatives every second,
They stayed there for more than ten years.

Fortunately, she had a mother with a pastry shop.
Capable, kind, tolerant, and very open-minded,
The middle-aged widow took care of the family and the shop,
Having raised three sons and one daughter, one by one.

The situation of the daughter's family concerned her.
She spread her warm embrace like a hen.
Ignoring other people's gossip, dissent, and criticism,
She kept the daughter's family close to her.

In order not to burden mom's family,
The daughter kept herself busy day and night,

Sewing clothes for people, stitch by stitch,
She gave her meager income to mother willingly.

Precautious, sensible, and eager to contribute, her two sons
did miscellaneous things at grandma and uncle's home.
Making tea cakes, whether frying or baking,
They were not afraid of hardship, tiredness, or sweating.

More than ten years passed,
Both sons had passed the age of marriage.
Their mother also aged,
Looking like an old woman.

Some government office wrote to seek an answer,
As Li Sheng had no friends or places to resort to.
Where he could stay would affect the rest of his life.
The best way out was to return to his original family.

The eldest sister gritted her teeth hearing about her husband
as for more than a decade, he neglected her and their kids,
disregarding her lack of mobility due to her bound feet, ignoring
the upbringing and growth of their two sons all along.

Fortunately, the Communist Party had led people to liberation,
The latter were given land and housing.
The elder son became the manager of a store,
The younger one honing his skills in a pastry workshop.

Leaves return to their roots, and water to the sea.
The strayed soul went back to its hometown;
After all, he was the father of their sons.
"Come home!" The eldest sister opened her forgiving arms!

Finally, the eldest sister established her own family.
Finally the husband and wife, and the father and sons reunited;
Li Sheng finally returned to his home, cleansing his soul
with repentance on each new step for the rest of his life.

乡政府看在眼里急在心里,
责怪老三无能也不争气,
在乡下重新盖房安置,
同小镇有五里左右的距离。

有人指着老三道出心声:
"共产党毛主席是你前世的父亲!"
老三噙眼交加悲喜交集,
五味杂陈的心情难以说清。

上有共产党毛主席,
子女们也听话也努力,
两儿上大学,小儿当局级干部,复旦大学教授,
孙辈有国外留学工作,有任大学老师,个个有出息。

老三临终前来不及表达自己的心愿,
其实是心中早想好的遗言:
遗产没有留下一分但比遗产更珍贵:
"子子孙孙要永远记住毛主席共产党的大恩大德,
     饮水要思源!"

= 完 =

Yutang Sang worked as an advanced news editor in the Xinjiang Radio and Television Bureau before retiring. He writes novels, essays, editorials, and jokes. In this creative volume, he recalls his hometown Shuangqiao in Zhangjiagang, Suzhou City, Jiangsu Province in China. He documents its prosperity, its tragedies, its colorful residents, historical events, and crucial institutions. The memoir is a beautiful combination of factual recollection and whimsical poetry drawing on both Yutang's memory as well as his imagination.

Dr. Yuan Sang works as a Chinese Mandarin instructor in the United States and enjoys building a bridge between English and Chinese cultures. She also writes fiction and non-fiction stories and produces Chinese music radio shows on KBGA.